HARBORS AND HIGH SEAS

ALSO BY DEAN KING

A Sea of Words:
A Lexicon and Companion
for Patrick O'Brian's
Seafaring Tales

DEAN KING

with John B. Hattendorf

Maps by William Clipson
and Adam Merton Cooper

HENRY HOLT AND COMPANY
NEW YORK

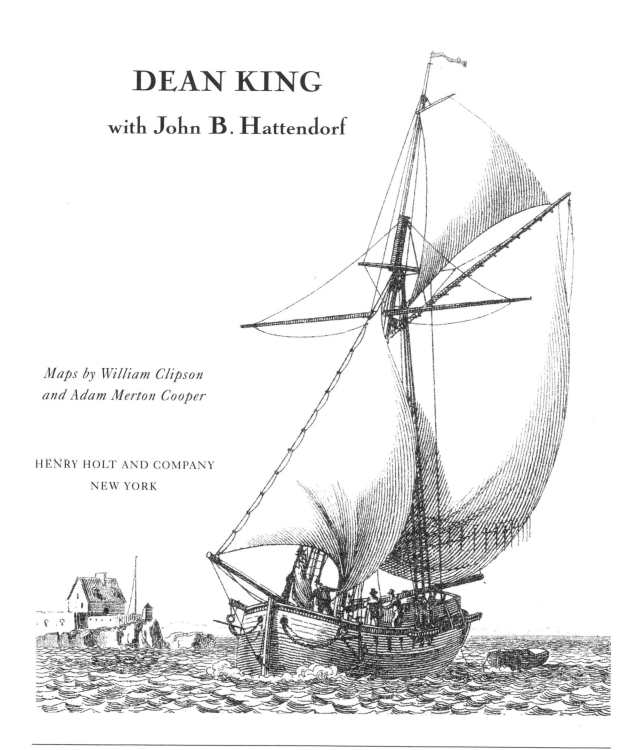

HARBORS
and
HIGH SEAS

✳

An Atlas and Geographical Guide to the

Aubrey-Maturin Novels of **PATRICK O'BRIAN**

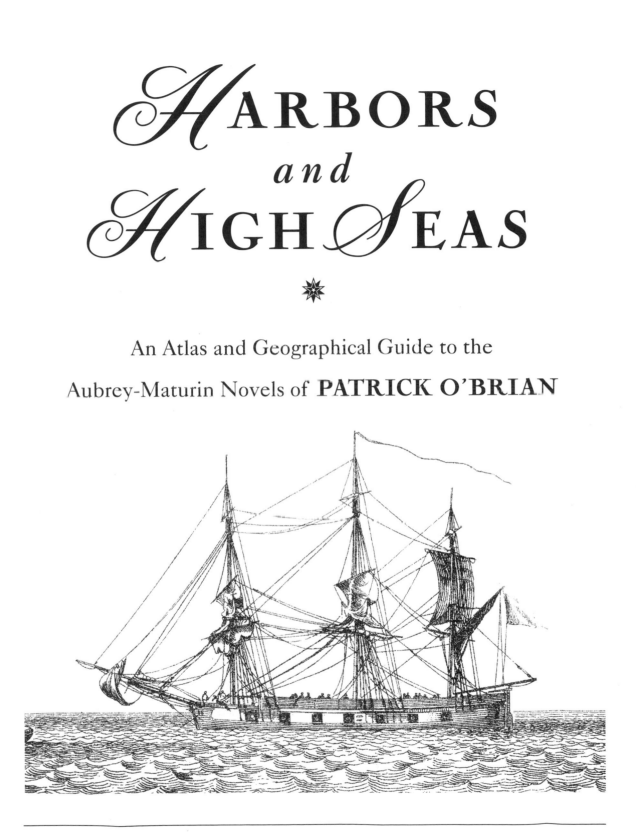

Henry Holt and Company, Inc.
Publishers since 1866
115 West 18th Street
New York, New York 10011

Henry Holt® is a registered trademark of Henry Holt and Company, Inc.

Published in Canada by Fitzhenry & Whiteside Ltd.,
195 Allstate Parkway, Markham, Ontario L3R 4T8.

Library of Congress Cataloging-in-Publication Data
King, Dean.
Harbors and high seas : an atlas and geographical guide to the Aubrey/Maturin
novels of Patrick O'Brian / Dean King with John B. Hattendorf ; maps by
William Clipson and Adam Merton Cooper.
p.   cm.
Includes bibliographical references (p.) and index.
1. O'Brian, Patrick, 1914–   —Knowledge—Geography.
2. Historical fiction, English—History and criticism.   3. Sea stories,
English—History and criticism.   4. Maturin, Stephen (Fictitious character)
5. Aubrey, Jack (Fictitious character) 6. Geography in literature.
7. Setting (Literature) I. Hattendorf, John B.   II. Clipson, William J.
III. Cooper, Adam Merton.   IV. Title.
PR6029.B55Z73   1996   96-6240
823'.914—dc20   CIP

ISBN 0-8050-4759-X
ISBN 0-8050-4610-0   (An Owl Book: pbk.)

Henry Holt books are available for special promotions and
premiums. For details contact: Director, Special Markets.

First Edition—1996

DESIGNED BY KATE NICHOLS

Illustrations appearing throughout book—Frontispiece: A cutter, commonly
called a sloop, seen from ahead. Title page: An armed pram (or lighter)
coming to anchor. Page 7: A French ship-rigged sloop getting underway.
Page 31: A spanish xebec (also called chebeck) with lateen sails, sailing before
the wind. Page 47: (*left*) A merchant vessel sailing before the wind with
studdingsails set; (*right*) a tartana sailing before the wind.

Printed in the United States of America
All first editions are printed on acid-free paper.∞

1   3   5   7   9   10   8   6   4   2

For Grace

Contents

Acknowledgments

I have the honor here to thank my entire crew for another glorious voyage. I cannot say too much in praise of Logan Ward, whose unfailing courage and spirited exertions in the smoky confusion of battle were beyond praise. To my wife, Jessica King, whose skillful penmanship, both editorial and illustrative, in the face of a blistering deadline was unmatched by the efforts of His Majesty's enemies, I render my sincerest compliments and thanks.

Much praise is due, likewise, to master mapmaker William Clipson, a salty dog without whose maps our striving would have been blind, and to the zealous Adam Merton Cooper, a fine young cartographer, who is as careful in his research as he is skilled in the newest charting techniques.

I beg leave also to praise Professor John B. Hattendorf, whose experience and erudition are the bedrock upon which many great works have been accomplished. To those at the Victualling and Ordnance Board, particularly David Sobel, Jonathan Swain Landreth, and Jody Rein, my utmost gratitude. I should also like to recognize those others who helped in many small ways, such as Joe Jackson, librarian of the New York Yacht Club; Saundra Taylor, curator of manuscripts at Lilly Library, Indiana University; Jerry Lamothe, head of graphics at the Naval War College in Newport; and the staffs of the New York Public Library and the Henry Eccles Library at the Naval War College in Newport. Also, Greg Easley, Jim Woollcombe, and Rob Mocatta (with whom I have rambled across England and on the South Downs, his home turf) and his wife Jane Mocatta, a barrister, for her information regarding the Temple. A glass of wine with you all!

—D.K.

HARBORS AND HIGH SEAS

Foreword

DEAN KING

If Stephen Maturin takes the fall for readers of Patrick O'Brian's Aubrey-Maturin novels regarding nautical terms, it is Sophie Williams who has that honor regarding geography. As with Maturin and ships, most readers readily empathize with Sophie's plight. In fact, it is with considerable relief that in *HMS Surprise* the reader hears her plead with Maturin, " 'I am sure there are quantities of young women who know where Pappenburg is, and Batavia, and this Ligurian Republic; but we never did such places with Miss Blake. And this Kingdom of Two Sicilies: I can find one on the map, but not the other. Stephen, pray tell me the present state of the world.' "

Maturin's succinct response to Sophie's plea, however, only touches on the complex geography of the era. Today, two centuries later, much more is needed. In fact, in our first companion book to O'Brian's novels, *A Sea of Words*, Professor John B. Hattendorf devoted ten pages to explaining the five different coalitions that formed to oppose French aggression during the War of the French Revolution (1792–1802) and the Napoleonic War (1803–1815). Not only did islands and territories change hands through battle and treaty, but when war broke out again in 1803, some exchanges were reversed and others were not. The Treaty of Amiens returned Minorca to Spain and the Cape of Good Hope to Holland. Britain later recaptured the Cape, and took Mauritius from the French, but never regained Minorca, although they sometimes operated from Port Mahon (the principal port of Minorca) anyway.

Readers of *A Sea of Words* indicated that the next most anxiously awaited tool for O'Brian aficionados was a book of maps. *Harbors and High Seas*—organized in seventeen chapters, one for each of the Aubrey-Maturin novels, and providing original and period maps, plus descriptions and engravings of many ports and coasts—is our answer. The purpose of this book is to help readers follow the geography of the action as it unfolds. For those who need to brush up on, say, the first dozen books before delving into the last handful, this book should also serve as a useful refresher. On the other hand, I have made a studious attempt to describe the plots, with salient information regarding ships and characters, without giving away endings.

✸

Little did I realize when I started working on *Harbors and High Seas* what a rewarding and often fiendish challenge it would be. The fiendish part was trying to locate in the oversize but often sparse atlases of the seventeenth, eighteenth, and nineteenth centuries the many obscure locales to which O'Brian sends Aubrey and Maturin and determining beyond a reasonable doubt which sites were fictional.

The rewarding parts were many. *A Sea of Words* contains the masses of information—about sailing and square-rigged ships, about Admiral Lord Nelson and the Royal Navy, and about many other nautical, natural science, and historical topics—that allow you to better understand the events of the Aubrey-Maturin novels. But *Harbors and High Seas* gives you the basis to truly absorb them. For the reader, geographic knowledge, like the keel and ribs of a ship, serves as a framework onto which all of the adventures, the humorous and poignant moments, the battles, can be fit.

After using this book, you will not only be able to envision the routes taken by the *Sophie*, the *Surprise*, or one of Captain Aubrey's temporary commands, but you will also better understand how the physical world was perceived during this era. Despite the advances made during the great age of discovery more than two centuries before, there were still plenty of uncharted—not to mention unfound—places. It's not surprising when you consider how rarely European traffic reached the remote parts of the world.

In his novel *The Unknown Shore*, O'Brian writes about St. Julian's, a harbor on the coast of Patagonia: "The first man ever to come there by sea, Magellan, built a gibbet on the shore and there hanged his mutineers; and Drake, coming there nearly sixty years after, did the same. So the creatures of this lost, ill-omened shore were used to strange things, whenever ships came in: the occasions were rare enough, for in the two centuries that separated Magellan from Mr. Anson only a score of ships had touched there . . ." (p. 148). And in *The Reverse of the Medal*, O'Brian informs us that "Jack had often travelled five thousand miles in quite frequented sea-lanes without seeing another ship."

Time and again this is illustrated in *The Naval Chronicle*, the journals published twice yearly from 1799 to 1818 detailing the naval actions of the Napoleonic wars and providing a forum for the discussion of maritime issues. Frequent hydrographic updates—and accounts of shipwrecks—prove just how necessary accurate sailing charts were and just how often they were not available. For instance, an 1814 edition reports: It would be of great benefit were the coast of Brazil to be surveyed from Demerary to Cape St. Roque, as no good charts exist of this part of the American coast, and even the cape that is the projecting angle of the continent and is fronted by a dangerous reef (Roccas) at the distance of several leagues seems not yet to be ascertained within twelve or fifteen miles of its true situation in latitude!*

Not only were many coasts still unexplored, but, as occurs so devastatingly in *The Wine Dark Sea*, new ones were forming. An account in the spring edition of *The Naval Chronicle* for 1812 tells of an island being formed in the Azores, an archipelago in the Atlantic Ocean off Portugal: When the *Sabrina* approached the volcano, it was still raging in the most awful manner, spewing large stones, cinders, and ashes from under water and sending shock waves to the ship with each explosion. At noon, the mouth of the crater emerged from the sea. The smoke drew up waterspouts that dissipated in a heavy rain, blanketing the *Sabrina*'s decks three miles away in fine black sand.

Two weeks later, the ship returned and found a new island, two miles around and quiet. A party from the ship landed on the steep shore to take possession of the isle in the name of His Britannic Majesty and to ascend the Atlantic's newest peak. On Sabrina, the crew found a large fuming basin, with a stream of boiling water flowing to the sea. The ascent of the two-hundred-foot peak was not easy. The sulfurous ground was so hot that once they reached the summit, they immediately descended and departed, the volcano belching smoke behind them.

The formation of terra firma out of the blue was an awesome event not lost on the intrepid crew of the *Sabrina*. Even though they had reason to believe the volcano might soon erupt again, they were determined to explore and to implant on Sabrina Island an English union jack in the name of their king. It is a telling event. In many ways, Aubrey and Maturin are the fictional embodiment of this spirit of discovery, this national pride, and this unadulterated gumption exhibited by the crew of the *Sabrina*.

✳

A few notes about using *Harbors and High Seas:* First of all, once again I had the privilege of turning to Professor Hattendorf, the Ernest J. King Professor of Maritime His-

* This excerpt is paraphrased, as are all of *The Naval Chronicle* excerpts in this book.

tory at the Naval War College in Newport, Rhode Island, with my innumerable questions, the answers to which and more you will find in his informative introduction to this book. If you wish to learn about the physical world, about the trade routes, winds, and tides, this is an excellent guide.

Second, the maps in the introduction and the general reference maps of Britain and Europe were drawn by Adam Merton Cooper. Following these, the seventeen chapters in *Harbors and High Seas*, which correspond to the Aubrey-Maturin books, contain route maps by Bill Clipson. To maximize the amount of information we could provide, places relevant to more than one book are often not repeated. For instance, many of the Spanish locations in book 17 are actually marked on a map of Spain in chapter 13. (By not creating another map of Spain, we were able to provide close-up looks at the West African coast and Ireland's southwest coast in chapter 17.) So, for places that you can't find in a given chapter, refer to the index.

Also, please note that the ship and other icons are merely illustrative art that will help you locate key sites. Obviously they are not to scale (or they would be invisible). As for the fictional sites marked on the various maps that appear in this book, they are approximations based on the evidence in the novels which is sometimes too vague for more than an informed guess. Moahu, for example, is in the Pacific Ocean somewhere between the Sandwich (Hawaiian) Islands and Christmas Island. Its exact placement on a map cannot be determined by the information given.

One note regarding the historic scenes and charts found in *Harbors and High Seas:* other than four prints from *Old London Taverns* (Brentano's, 1901), these are taken from the forty volumes of *The Naval Chronicle*. The captions that accompany them also come from *The Naval Chronicle*. They have been edited, sometimes heavily, for clarity and brevity. Other excerpts from *The Naval Chronicle* have also frequently been heavily edited. In citing the various volumes, for convenience I have called the January-to-June edition of each year the "spring" edition and the July-to-December edition the "fall" edition.

✸

And by the way, Pappenburg was a city in the Grande Duchy of Ahremburg (today part of Germany), near the Ems River and the Dutch border; Batavia (today Djakarta) was the major city and port of Java in the Dutch East Indies; the Ligurian Republic, which existed from 1797 to 1805, was a strip of coast surrounding Genoa; and the Kingdom of Two Sicilies, which appears on some period maps and not on others—from 1806 to 1815 it was known as the Kingdom of Naples—was formed of southern Italy and the island of Sicily.

Finally, sad to say, the great island of Sabrina suffered a rather swift demise despite its two-mile shoreline and two-hundred-foot peak, though its creation was not entirely for naught. According to *The Naval Chronicle*, the islet of Sabrina "gradually disappeared . . . leaving an extensive shoal."

INTRODUCTION

Not a Moment to Lose

John B. Hattendorf

To the landsman, navigating the oceans can seem a mystifying endeavor—particularly with respect to the Age of Sail, when uncharted reefs and lee shores often meant sudden death to the misguided or unlucky ship. In those days, signing on as a seaman was an act of faith. Belief in the captain's skills had to be total.

For the captain, guiding a wooden ship halfway around the world was also, in many senses, an act of faith—in his own talent as well as in the goodwill of nature. The captain's decisions could alter the course of a voyage in the most momentous way, such as in 1788 when, in the stormy seas surrounding Cape Horn and pelted by hail and sleet, Captain Bligh put the ship about, deciding to sail around the world in the *other* direction.

Of course, as Sir John Barrow recounts in *The Mutiny of the Bounty*, Bligh had some compelling reasons to make that decision: "the ship began to complain, and required pumping every hour; the decks became so leaky that the commander was obliged to allot the great cabin to those who had wet berths, to hang their hammocks in. Finding they were losing ground every day, and that it was hopeless to persist in attempting a passage by this route, at this season of the year, to the Society Islands, and after struggling for thirty days in this tempestuous ocean, it was determined to bear away for the Cape of Good Hope . . . to the great joy of every person on board" (p. 41).

No matter what the conditions, it took an extraordinary man, endowed with a special intellect, intuition, and resolve, to make and answer for such a decision. To comprehend and calculate innumerable variables, to study charts and relate that sometimes flawed information with the physical clues around him—the color and temperature of the ocean, the altitude of the sun and stars, the appearance of an albatross, perhaps—became, in essence, a sixth sense.

As Stephen Maturin blithely states in *The Letter of Marque*, " 'I believe . . . that to the mariner paths are stretched across the ocean according to the wind and weather: these he follows with as little thought or concern as a Christian might walk down Sackville Street, cross Carlisle Bridge, pass Trinity College and so come to Stephen's Green, that haunt of dryads, each more elegant than the last.' " While Maturin's tongue-in-cheek appreciation of navigation on the high seas—likening it to a simple walk through the streets of Dublin—also gives him the irresistibly delightful opportunity to backhandedly suggest that Aubrey might be something other than Christian, it also contains more than a modicum of truth. Maturin's mind simply wanders whenever Aubrey begins calculating routes, particularly when the probable route of an enemy also must be factored into the equation.

Long removed from that age, most of us can hardly imagine the difficulties of operating so complicated, so awkward, and so intricate a piece of engineering as a tall-masted sailing ship on an ocean voyage. By the time of the Napoleonic wars, the arts of navigation and seamanship were based on some of the most advanced scientific and technological concepts of the day. The roots of these fundamentals can be traced back to classical knowledge, gaining headway in the technological revolution born of the first great age of discovery during the fifteenth and sixteenth centuries, when courageous navigators explored the Atlantic and Indian oceans. By the end of the eighteenth century, European seamen were participating in the second age of discovery, which focused on the little-known expanses of the Pacific.

The captain of a large sailing ship needed skills and experience in two broad areas, requiring quite different types of knowledge. First, he had to know his ship—how to operate and repair her rigging and sails, how to care for the health and morale of her men, and how to maintain and use her charts, logs, navigational instruments, and guns. Second, he had to be a ship handler and voyager who knew how to make the best use of winds and ocean currents all over the world. With practical experience, one could learn the first specialty in half a dozen years. The second, however, took half a lifetime to master. It was an education that began almost as soon as a son was born to a mariner or, if not then, when he was sent away as a ship's boy, not yet a teenager. It was necessarily a long tradition of seafaring that helped inculcate these skills in each new generation.

Today we would classify the different types of knowledge that a master mariner needed under such categories as maritime meteorology, cartography, and hydrography.

Knowledge in these areas developed gradually and was much more rudimentary than it is today.

WINDS AND WEATHER

Because wind was the fundamental source of power in a sailing vessel, a seaman needed to know as much as possible about its patterns around the globe, patterns that had been discovered only by trial and error. By the late eighteenth century, mariners clearly understood the general pattern of the winds and how to use them, if not fully their causes.

We know today that winds are fundamentally the movement of the earth's atmosphere, which by its weight exerts a pressure on the earth that we can measure using a barometer. The globe is divided into relatively permanent bands of different atmospheric pressures. At the two poles these bands exert more, or higher, pressure than the mean pressure. At the equator it is lower than the mean. Between the polar highs and the equatorial low, there are two more bands of permanent pressure differences, one high and the other low.

The high and low bands of pressure create movement in the atmosphere—wind. This wind draws from the center of a high-pressure area toward the center of a low-pressure area. Because of the earth's rotation, this movement of the atmosphere is deflected in a clockwise direction in the northern hemisphere and in a counter-clockwise direction in the southern hemisphere. Thus, on each side of the different bands, the wind blows in a different direction. There is little wind near the center. At the equator the low-pressure area is called the "doldrums." It is a region where there is generally little wind, but where one can also encounter the occasional squall or thunderstorm, or even hurricanes at certain times of year. On the two outer sides of that band, in a broad region where the low- and high-pressure bands meet, the winds are known as "trade winds," or "trades," a term that comes not from any reference to commerce but from the expression "to blow trade," meaning to blow regularly.

The two trade winds are affected by the same equatorial low pressure, but being on different sides of the equator, the earth's rotation causes the northern trade to blow from the northeast and the southern one to blow from the southeast. Higher, toward each of the poles, the prevailing winds blow from the west and thus are called the "westerlies." Between them and the trade winds are areas of light winds called the "variables." They were also known as the "horse latitudes" because of the ill—and

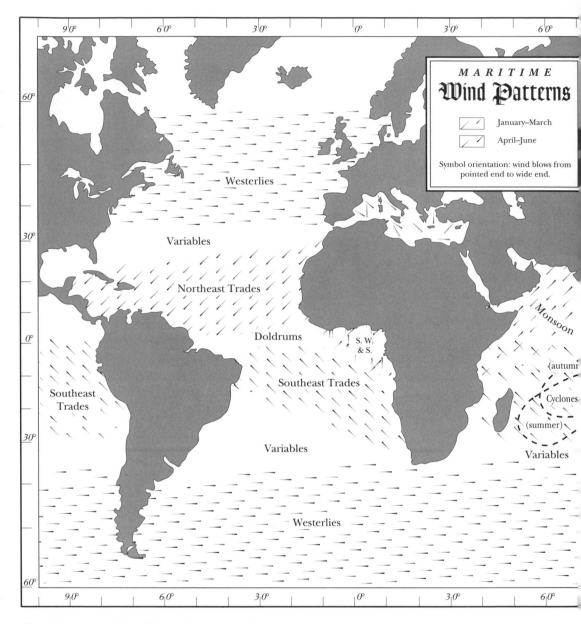

Neat Diagram of the Winds: January to June. This chart of maritime wind patterns shows the general expected wind directions (the indicators are wider in the direction the wind is blowing) at certain times of year. But as Aubrey once chided Maturin in the book *Desolation Island:* " 'these neat diagrams of the winds were all very fine and large, but he [Maturin] must not run away with the

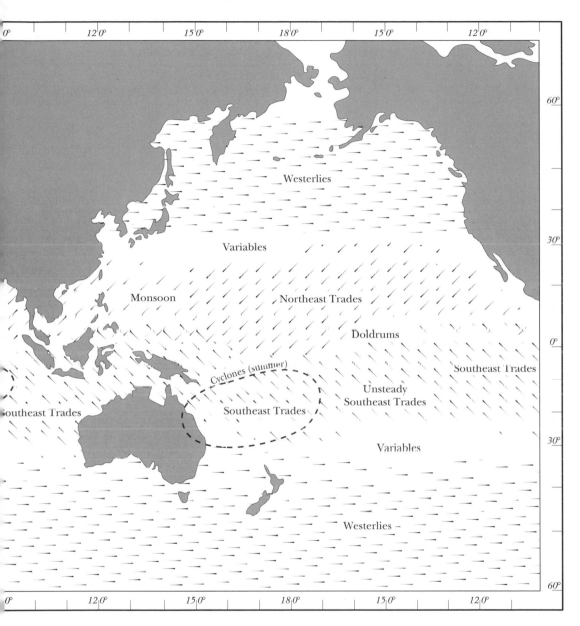

idea that nature copied books, or that as soon as the trades left off, the westerlies set in: above all in a year like this, when the south-easter did not reach nearly as far beyond the line as they had had a right to expect—there was no telling just what winds they should find a little farther east of south.' "
NOTE: Keep in mind that the seasons are reversed in the southern hemisphere.

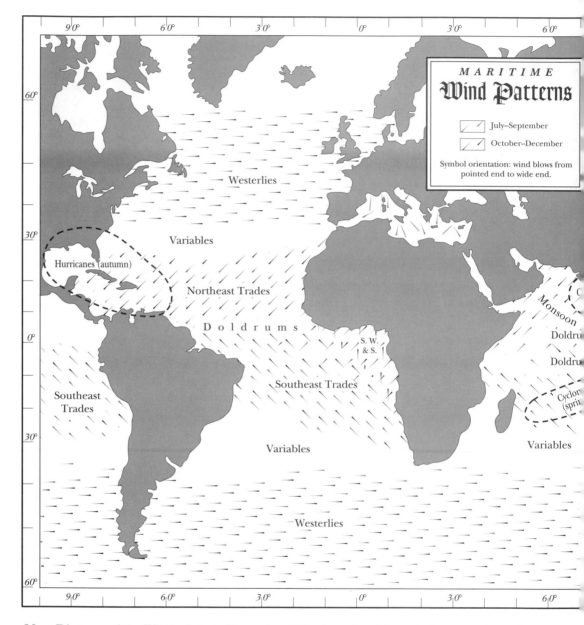

Neat Diagram of the Winds: July to December. This chart of maritime wind patterns shows the general expected wind directions (the indicators are wider in the direction the wind is blowing) at certain times of the year.

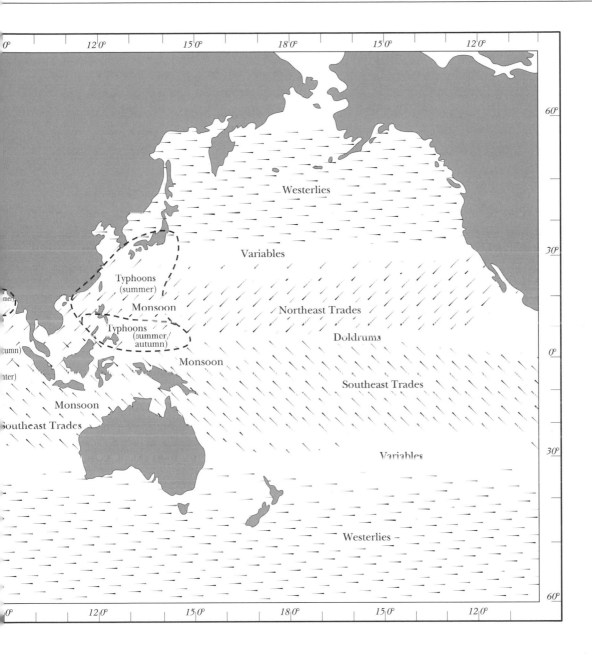

often fatal—effect that the lack of wind and stifling heat had on horses being transferred to America.

These general features govern the basic wind patterns at sea, but they can be altered by a number of factors. Among the most important is the presence of land. The band of high pressure at about 30°N latitude splits into two separate areas of high pressure in the eastern Atlantic, one near the Canary Islands and another in the eastern Pacific, off California. Likewise, the belt of low pressure at 60°N latitude concentrates near Iceland and near the Aleutian Islands. In the southern hemisphere, where no such land masses are present, the low-pressure belt is relatively uniform around the globe.

In addition, high-pressure systems tend to form over land masses in winter and low-pressure ones in summer due to temperature variations. This seasonal change is what creates monsoons in the Indian Ocean. Another seasonal change is the shifting of various prevailing winds according to the sun's movement in relation to the tropics. The northeast trade winds, for example, shift between 28° and 3°N latitude from June to September.

Although the eighteenth-century mariner did not know all of the reasons for these wind changes, he did have a clear understanding of the general pattern of winds. Such knowledge was crucial for the captain of a square-rigged ship, primarily because he needed to keep the wind astern or abeam, where his ship was designed to accept the wind's stress and her sails worked most efficiently. To maintain his ship in the correct semicircle of the wind, he had to remain constantly alert to its nuances and be able to predict its next move. The masts were not supported for winds from ahead. In such winds, the yards could not be easily moved and many sails could not be used or were subject to damage.

While the mariner of the day did not have all the accurate scientific explanations for the wind and weather, he was well equipped with long-standing practical advice. For example, changes in the glass—or barometric pressure—were interpreted by these seaman's ditties:

First rise after low,
foretells stronger blow.

Or even more bluntly,

With rising wind and falling glass,
soundly sleeps the silly ass.

The global wind patterns were the basis for trade routes. On the high seas of the Atlantic, Pacific, and Indian oceans, a captain could not merely set sail in a certain compass direction, as he often could do in coastal passages or in seas such as the Baltic, the Channel, or the Mediterranean, which were within one band of wind and influenced by continental weather patterns. To make the best passage to a distant point across the ocean, a mariner followed a circuitous route, keyed to the prevailing winds.

OCEAN CURRENTS

Another major factor affecting long voyages was ocean currents. While these currents occur at different depths in the sea, the surface current is usually the only one that affects sailing ships. Surface currents are created mainly by the prevailing winds, primarily the trade winds in the two hemispheres. In both the Atlantic and the Pacific oceans, the trades push an enormous body of water westward across more than fifty degrees of latitude, broken only by the relatively narrow equatorial and polar countercurrents. Moving in a clockwise direction north of the equator, and counterclockwise south of the equator, these currents, together with the branches and eddies that spring from them, can either hinder or assist ships.

There are two types of surface currents. One type flows east or west and has a temperature that matches the climate of its latitude. The second type runs north or south and is usually either warmer or colder than the climate in the same area. Currents that transport warm water to higher latitudes begin on the western side of each of the ocean systems. Examples are the Gulf Stream in the North Atlantic, the Brazil Current in the South Atlantic, and the Mozambique and Agulhas Currents in the Indian Ocean. The Canary Current in the North Atlantic and the Benguela Current in the South Atlantic both transport cold water on the east side of an ocean system. The Indian Ocean has no similar upwelling because no large land mass blocks the water flow.

The cold currents that originate in high latitudes are of particular concern to navigators since they can create fog and poor visibility or even carry ice to lower latitudes, as occurs in *The Wine Dark Sea* when the *Surprise* rounds Cape Horn and encounters treacherous ice islands. The strength of these currents normally varies from less than a quarter of a knot to less than three knots. In recent times, the strongest ocean currents in the world have been observed south of the island of Socotra in the Indian Ocean, where the Somali current reaches seven knots during the height of the southwest monsoon. Other local currents are caused by tidal conditions, differences in water temperature, and storms.

FAVORED ROUTES

Master mariners came to understand that each ocean had its own peculiarities and patterns. For example, the Portuguese explorers of the fifteenth century were the first to discover that the best route to India was to sail first toward the coast of Brazil, then to recross the Atlantic and sail toward the tip of southern Africa. With experience, mariners also learned that at various times of the year, a certain area in the mid-Atlantic, sometimes nearer the Brazilian coast than the African coast, allowed ships to pass quickly through the doldrums.

In trying to find this elusive area, a mariner had to be careful not to work too far to the west, where he might be swept by the current into the Caribbean, or too far east, where the Gulf of Guinea on the African coast awaited with its contrary winds. Having successfully negotiated the doldrums, the ship made its southing on the southeast trade winds, and then the Brazil current speeded her west to the Cape of Good Hope.

The changes in seasonal winds and weather often dictated the times at which ships set out on long voyages. Toward the end of the eighteenth century, for example, merchant ships sailing for the Far East tended to leave their home ports between April and June.

The Atlantic

For those crossing the Atlantic at most times of the year, even from England and northern Europe, the best route—with the best weather and the most dependable wind—was usually close to the one Columbus used. Leaving the English Channel, they sailed as far to the west as possible to avoid being pushed by currents into the difficult waters of the Bay of Biscay. It was particularly important to clear, and not even to sight, if possible, Ushant, the rocky island off the northwestern corner of France. Then, when the wind began to veer more westerly, the seaman set a more southerly course to pass Cape Finesterre on the northwestern coast of Spain with ample room, sailing to the west of the island of Madeira and then changing course to pass to the west and in sight of the Cape Verde Islands.

A more northern route to the Grand Banks was shorter by a thousand miles but safely used only in autumn, when the ice had melted. Most vessels preferred the longer, safer voyage, avoiding the frequent fog and ice off the Newfoundland banks.

Indian Ocean

In the Indian Ocean, vessels usually sailed directly east from the Cape of Good Hope along latitude 40°S, passing the islands of St. Paul and Amsterdam about halfway, then turned either north for the Dutch East Indies and the South China Sea or northwest for India and Ceylon, the timing of the voyage carefully planned according to the destination. After failing to round Cape Horn, Bligh chose this eastern route in the *Bounty*, eventually sailing south of New Holland (Australia) and New Zealand before heading north to Tahiti.

Ships heading for Ceylon and India between July and January could pass between the southeastern coast of Africa and the island of Madagascar. On the return journey from India or the Dutch East Indies, ships usually sailed past Mauritius and then on to the Cape of Good Hope, turning north in the Atlantic and calling at St. Helena, Ascension Island, the Cape Verde Islands, or the Azores, before heading for home ports.

The Mediterranean

The Mediterranean presented quite a different picture for navigation. Its narrow length constricted in the center by Sicily, Italy, and Malta creates two major basins. The Aegean, Ionian, Adriatic, and Tyrrhenian seas each have their particular characteristics as well. Nevertheless, cruising the length of the Mediterranean, confined as it is along a relatively narrow band of latitude, did not involve dealing with as many changing wind patterns as did sailing the oceans. Notwithstanding various currents and occasional hazards and shallows, one could often sail fairly directly from one port to another.

Some broad patterns were discernible. For example, during the summer months, in sailing from Gibraltar to Malta, a seaman steered midway between Spain and Africa until reaching Cape de Gata at the southeastern tip of Spain, then followed the African coast, taking advantage of the west winds and the east-running current, to sail directly for Malta. In winter, however, strong northwest winds make the African coast a dangerous lee shore, so ships headed to safer waters farther offshore. They generally sailed from Cape de Gata to the southern coast of Sardinia, then proceeded along the northern side of the Strait of Sicily to Malta.

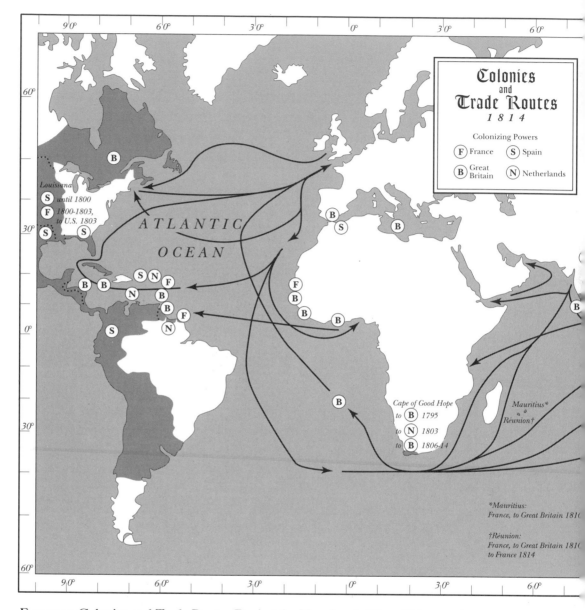

European Colonies and Trade Routes During the Napoleonic Wars. This map gives a general picture of the colonial possessions of the major European powers during the Napoleonic wars and tells the years of some key changes in possession. In addition, it delineates some of the principal world trade routes, along which privateers and Naval warships could also be expected to cruise.

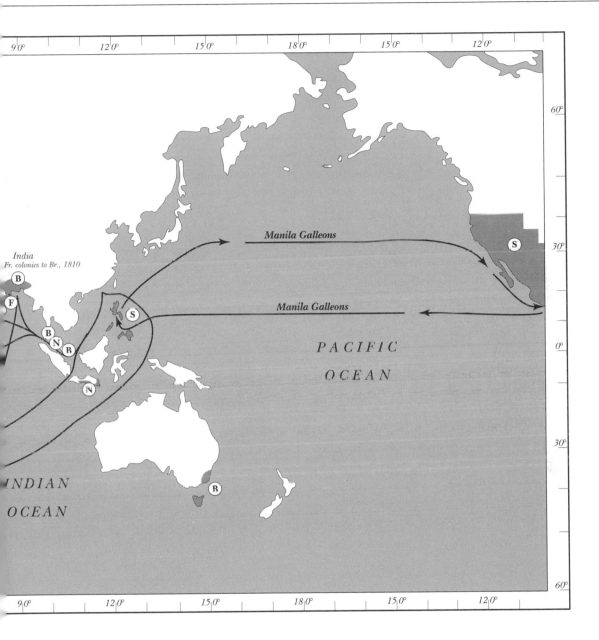

LENGTH OF VOYAGES

As we have seen, a straight line was usually neither the quickest nor the best route for a long passage. And with so many factors at play, every journey was unique. Even if they had smooth passages, two seaworthy vessels could make the same long voyage at very different speeds. But one can get a good idea of the time required for a long voyage by looking at the records of merchant vessels, which depended on a relatively timely return. In the middle of the eighteenth century, for example, three-decker Swedish East India Company ships sailing to China took an average of a year and seven months (591 days) to make the round-trip between Europe and China. Part of that time was spent shipping cargo, waiting for good weather, or refitting or resupplying en route, at places such as St. Helena, Ascension Island, or Cape Town; but even discounting these in-port days, they still averaged more than a year (383 days) at sea.

Likewise, Dutch ships in the late eighteenth century took an average of 124 days to sail from Holland to Cape Town and 117 days to return home. This is roughly the amount of time it would have taken a British warship, such as the *Surprise,* to make the same journey.

DUTCH EAST INDIA COMPANY SHIPS, 1790–95

Dutch ships began making regular voyages to Asia in 1595, and from 1602, nearly all of the vessels were outfitted by the Dutch East India Company. Over the decades, the Dutch compiled much statistical data regarding these expeditions. The following figures provide a valuable guideline for estimating the length of voyages during this period. Because the Dutch preferred the slower shallow draft ships necessary in their home waters, however, Aubrey's passage would have been slightly faster than those shown here.

Voyage (one-way)	Distance in Nautical Miles	Average Number of Days Under Sail	Average Day's Sail in Nautical Miles
Holland to Cape Town	8,000	129	62
Cape Town to Batavia	6,450	85	76
Cape Town to Ceylon	6,750	97	69
Batavia to Cape Town	5,900	89	66
Ceylon to Cape Town	5,500	64	86
Cape Town to Holland	7,500	117	64

Source: J. R. Bruijn et al., eds., *Dutch-Asiatic Shipping in the 17th and 18th Centuries* (The Hague: Martinus Nijhoff, 1987), tables 6, 11, 15, 20.

NORTH ATLANTIC SAILING PACKETS, 1818–32

In the years just after the Napoleonic War, ships began making regularly scheduled and very swift crossings of the North Atlantic. While they did not approach the speeds of the clipper ships that followed several decades later, the packets that sailed from 1818 to 1832 do give us an idea of the time it took ships in Aubrey's day to cross the North Atlantic. The season of the year made a difference in the amount of time required and the optimum route. In the early part of the year, a more direct route was possible, while in spring and summer, one had to take a longer detour to the south in order to avoid ice produced by the melting polar cap and fog caused by the warm weather.

VOYAGE	DISTANCE IN NAUTICAL MILES	FASTEST CROSSING	SLOWEST CROSSING
New York to Liverpool	2,996 (winter)-3,148 (spring)	21 days	29 days
Liverpool to New York	3,540 (winter)-3,723 (summer)	34 days	46 days

SOURCE: R. G. Albion, *Square Riggers on Schedule* (Princeton, N.J.: Princeton University Press, 1938), pp. 9–11, 191, 322.

NELSON'S CHASE OF VILLENEUVE, 1805

Among the famous events leading up to the Battle of Trafalgar in October 1805 was Nelson's dramatic search for his opponent, Admiral Villeneuve. At one point, while Napoleon was contemplating the invasion of England, Villeneuve attempted to lure the British fleet away from Europe. He sailed for the West Indies with Nelson chasing him and returned to Europe a month later with Nelson still in pursuit. Nelson's fast voyage to the West Indies provides us with a good example of what a naval fleet could do in crossing the Atlantic while pressing on all sail.

VOYAGE	DISTANCE IN NAUTICAL MILES	NUMBER OF DAYS UNDER SAIL	AVERAGE DAY'S SAIL IN NAUTICAL MILES
Cape St. Vincent to Barbados	3,227	24	134.5
Barbados to Cape St. Vincent	3,459	38	91
Cape Spartel to Ushant	1,800	21	85.7

SOURCE: Julian S. Corbett, *The Campaign of Trafalgar*, vol. 1 (London: Longman's Green, 1919), charts between pages 170–71, 204–5; and Geoffrey Rawson, ed., *Letters from Lord Nelson* (London and New York: Staples Press, 1949), p. 442.

SURVEYING THE SEAS

From his early days as a midshipman, Aubrey clearly relished surveying and charting coastal areas, a skill that serves him well later. In *The Letter of Marque*, while planning a cutting-out expedition, for example, he is able to produce a survey of a relevant section of French coast that he assisted in making in 1797 with "the master of the *Bellerophon*, the best hydrographer in the Navy."

Indeed, progress in navigational science was highly dependent on the observations that seamen brought home. Captain James Cook was one of the masters of this art, and much was learned from his example. Typically, when mariners neared a strange coast, they sketched plans and elevations. Cook systematized this practice by adapting methods used by army engineers on shore. Captain Murdoch Mackenzie used this approach in his 1774 *Treatise of Marine Surveying*, the first textbook on the subject. It remained the standard for many years.

Mackenzie also developed an instrument for surveying called a station pointer. With this the mariner could find the location of his vessel or a position ashore by using three objects whose positions were already established on an accurate chart. He could also use it to draft a chart of a newly surveyed area, such as a harbor, island, or coastline, incorporating both prominent landmarks and lead-line soundings.

To link this detailed information to the large-scale charts showing wide areas of the ocean, the seaman needed to establish the latitude and longitude of the position from which he was working. This step involved celestial observation. In *HMS Surprise*, while some of Aubrey's officers and men survey the harbor and anchorage of a remote and uninhabited island in the Indian Ocean, he and Stourton determine the longitude by observing the distance between the moon and Venus.

NAVIGATING AT SEA

While knowledge of mathematics, astronomy, and maritime instrument technology had advanced considerably by the early nineteenth century, mariners still faced great difficulties. A sailor was still at the mercy of wind and weather. To use science and technology to their greatest effect, a seaman had to employ his books and instruments when the sun, moon, and stars were in the most advantageous positions. High seas, wind, rain, snow, and clouds were not always accommodating. The mariner needed to locate his position whenever his situation required it, not just when the stars and planets were lined up to give it under perfect weather conditions.

Even when conditions were perfect, the most advanced approaches required erudition in mathematics and science. Few at sea had such preparation, and not everyone could afford the newest instruments. Others, out of habit, apathy, or plain suspicion, continued to use antiquated instruments and methods long after better ones were available. In the 1880s Captain Lecky, the author of a navigation manual, remarked: "There is, unfortunately, among sailors a very general and most erroneous notion that stellar observations and their calculations are something much too high and mighty to be tackled by ordinary mortals." It was something within the reach of all who chose to try, he argued. "There are, however, men afloat who won't try, and who for downright, double-barrelled, copper-bottomed, bevel-edged bigotry are matchless in all other professions" (*A History of the Practice of Navigation*, pp. 104–5).

An ordinary merchant master of this time would probably use a combination of dead reckoning and celestial navigation. He might take the bearing of his last departure point from land and then estimate his position by log line and courses sailed, combined with noontime sightings of the meridian altitude of the sun or, at night, observations of Polaris for latitude, and, when a chronometer was available, observations of the sun to find the longitude. Occasionally natural features could help him. In the North Atlantic, for example, some mariners in the late eighteenth century judged their longitude by the Gulf Stream, which they recognized by the lighter color of the water and its warmer temperature. Many still found their way by the old method of "running down the latitude," or placing the ship along the desired parallel of latitude and sailing along it until reaching their destination.

The difficulties involved in finding longitude were reflected by discrepancies on the charts. Mariners regularly recorded sightings of newly found islands and promontories, but they were often seen under poor conditions or without the facts necessary to determine their longitudes. Thus, there is a long history of lost islands, places that could not be found after their initial discovery. These same islands often moved about from one chart to another, creating great confusion. This was the case in *Desolation Island* as Aubrey, trying to locate Kerguelen Island, also known as Desolation Island, studies previous reports that the explorers Kerguélen-Trémarec and James Cook had made in the 1770s. There are numerous cases of this in the Pacific Ocean as well, perhaps the most famous of which is Pitcairn Island. The inaccurate plotting of that island's position in 1767 was one of the principal reasons why the mutineers from HMS *Bounty* escaped rediscovery for so many years.

The Tools of Navigation

The tools of navigation for explorers in the fifteenth and sixteenth centuries had been rudimentary, but by the time of the French Revolution and the Napoleonic War, technology had advanced considerably. However, the latest technology was too expensive for many seafarers. It was not uncommon to find old instruments, such as the octant and backstaff, that had been used more than a century before still in use even though more refined instruments had superseded them. For navigation on a long voyage, the typical mariner of Jack Aubrey's time might include among his tools a compass, charts, a pair of dividers, an instrument to take sights on stars or planets, a sandglass, a log line, a lead line, a chronometer, a Gunter's scale, and a traverse board.

Lead Line. The oldest of all navigational instruments, a lead line was a heavy weight, often made of lead, attached to a long line marked with the depth of the water. On the bottom of the lead there was a soft piece of tallow that could pick up samples of the sea bottom. With this tool, the navigator could find the depth of the water and determine the nature of the sea floor. These facts provided the experienced navigator with valuable information as to his location. For example, a mud bottom might show that one was near the mouth of a river, whereas coral could indicate a nearby reef or island. Mariners learned that particular types of bottom materials were found in particular places, and this information was often recorded on charts.

With a lead weighing 10 to 12 pounds, a seaman standing forward in the ship could cast the lead every few minutes as the ship sailed onward and call out the depth of the water. Weights of 18 to 24 pounds were used for depths of more than 100 fathoms. They normally required a winch, heavier lines, and cessation of the ship's forward motion. In 1800, however, an instrument maker in Newcastle invented a device that automatically locked and marked the line when the lead hit bottom, allowing a ship to continue sailing while sounding greater depths; however, at very great depths in the open ocean, the buoyancy of the line offset the weight and prevented soundings.

Compass. Although a compass is the navigator's most vital piece of equipment, the traditional compass became inadequate for his needs in the eighteenth and early nineteenth centuries. In the early 1700s, mariners had realized that there was a natural variation in the earth's magnetic field that prevented a compass from pointing toward true north. By the late eighteenth century, the increasing use of iron on ships made matters worse. British Naval Captain Matthew Flinders was the first person to explain this phenomenon. While surveying in HMS *Reliance* off Tasmania in 1798, he discovered that the errors changed when the ship changed course. In 1803 Flinders, unaware that war had recently been declared with France, touched at Mauritius, a French possession. Made a prisoner of war for more than six years, he put his idle time to good use by developing his theory on compass errors. Although he reported his scientific findings to the Royal Society and although in 1812 the *Naval Chronicle* published his suggestion that a compass could be corrected by adding a bar of iron (known as a "Flinders Bar" and still in use), no general change was made to compasses until decades after his death in 1814.

Charts. At one time, accurate sea and coastal charts were so hard-won and so valuable that they were considered by some nations to be state secrets. During the seventeenth and eighteenth centuries, however, private Dutch and English engravers published atlases and charts for use at sea. In England, the most famous of these firms during the 1790–1815 period included William Faden, Laurie and Wittle, J. W. Norie, and Aaron Arrowsmith.

Following the lead of the French Navy, which established its Depôt des Cartes et Plans in 1720, the Admiralty created the Hydrography Department in 1795 to carry out surveys at sea, to collate authoritative information for its own use and for chart publishers, and to publish its own charts. The first head of this office was the civilian hydrographer Alexander Dalrymple, who was previously the first hydrographer of the East India Company.

During the early stages of the Napoleonic wars, the Admiralty realized that more ships were being lost to inadequate charts than to the enemy. In 1800 the Hydrography Department published the first Admiralty charts. Using copperplate printing presses for fast production, Captain Thomas Hurd, Hydrographer of the Navy in 1808, equipped Naval captains with more and better charts than ever before.

Around this time, the Admiralty also undertook a number of surveys. From 1795 to 1798, Commander William Broughton surveyed in Japanese and Korean waters. Graeme Spencer surveyed the southern coast of England in 1800. Captain Matthew Flinders worked in Australia between 1801 and 1803. Francis Beaufort accompanied an expedition to the River Plate (between Argentina and Uruguay) in 1807 and completed a survey in those waters before turning his attention to the southern coast of Turkey in 1811 and 1812. William Smyth began a survey of the Adriatic in 1811 that would last many years.

Just as Bligh, even during his desperate open-boat voyage, accurately surveyed parts of the coast of Australia, and the fictional Aubrey assists various masters in the Royal Navy in surveying harbors and bays, many other hydrographer-seamen contributed valuable small-scale surveys to the mass of information compiled by the Hydrography Department.

Divider and Parallel Ruler. A navigator used a divider, which is a V-shaped instrument similar to a drawing compass, to determine distances on a chart, picking off the distance between two points on the chart and comparing it to the scale of miles. He could also use it to lay out the arc of angles taken from celestial observations. Using parallel rulers and a chart's compass rose, he could determine the compass course to steer.

Instruments for Sighting Stars. The oldest and simplest instruments used for taking the altitude of the sun, a planet, or a star in order to determine position at sea were the cross-staff and backstaff, measuring sticks with one or more sliding crosspieces made of wood, ivory, or ebony. Favorites of seamen beginning in the sixteenth century and still used in the early nineteenth century, these uncomplicated wooden instruments were used to determine latitude by "shooting" the altitude of the sun or the North Star.

Aubrey, however, uses an octant or sextant. With a small fixed telescope for observing a star and small movable mirrors attached to a scale, the octant (or Hadley's quadrant)—produced commercially beginning in 1731—improved the accuracy of sightings. The scale, one-eighth of the circumference of a circle, allowed measurement of angles up to 90 degrees. With an octant, a seaman could readily measure angles even in rough weather, as long as he could hold the instrument in a vertical position. British Naval Captain (later Rear Admiral) John Campbell later developed a more accurate instrument that could read angles up to 120 degrees. Much in use during Aubrey's day, it was called a sextant because its scale was on an arc that was one-sixth of the circumference of a circle.

Books of Tables and Sailing Directions. A "rutter," or book of sailing directions describing harbors and routes, contained information on prominent landmarks, sea bottom characteristics, shoals, and so forth. One such rutter, popular during the eighteenth century and regularly revised until about 1780, was the *English Pilot,* published by Mount and Page. It provided common sailing directions, atlases, and detailed charts. The East India Company also began to publish pilot books compiled by James Horsburgh. Updating some of these standard works at the end of the eighteenth century, William Norman published A *Pilot for the West Indies.* At the same time, Captain Edmund Furlong published the first edition of *The American Coast Pilot* at Newburyport, Massachusetts. This work eventually became a government publication and the modern *United States Coast Pilot.* But it wasn't until 1829 that the Admiralty began to publish sailing directions in the series of pilot books that continues today.

Books provided a variety of other information necessary for practical navigation at sea. Almanacs with tables for the declination of the sun were published as early as the fifteenth century. A century later such tables also included the positions of the prominent fixed stars. By 1600 there were also amplitude tables, giving the bearings of sunrise and sunset at various latitudes and allowing the mariner to check his compass for magnetic variation. Soon after, sailors began to use trigonometry and then logarithms to measure the angles of celestial bodies in determining their positions.

In 1763 England's future astronomer royal, Nevil Maskelyne, added to the bulk of tables with his *British Mariner's Guide* for taking lunar distances, using observations compiled by Professor Tobias Mayer of the University of Göttingen in Hanover. Connected with this was the process of comparing sightings of lunar events, such as an eclipse, the passage of Venus across the moon, or as Aubrey does in *HMS Surprise*, the occulations of Jupiter's moons. The difference in the times when such an event occurs in two different places—followed by a full page of handwritten calculations—could provide the mariner with the longitudinal difference between the two places.

Gunter's Scale. Also known as "Sliding Gunters," these were the forerunners of the slide rule. Seamen who were poorly educated in mathematics often preferred the mechanical aid of a Gunter to using tables. In 1803 the author of *The Geometrical Seaman* wrote, "Of all the different methods that have hitherto been proposed for performing the various practical operations in Navigation, . . . the Sliding Gunter is the easiest and at the same time sufficiently accurate for common practice" (p. 75).

Log Line. Early seamen estimated their speed by tossing a chip of wood overboard and repeating a ditty to measure the time it took to go the length of the ship. Improving upon this method in about 1570, English seamen invented the log line, a triangular piece of wood weighted at the lower edge with lead and attached to a line with knots originally at every seven fathoms (42 feet). A half-minute (more precisely a twenty-eight-second) sandglass was used to measure time as the knots that passed over the side as the line paid out were counted. The result gave the speed of the ship in nautical miles per hour. In 1756 astronomers revised the length of the nautical mile from 5,000 feet to 6,080 feet. Ever conservative, navigators eventually altered the interval between the knots on the log line to correspond with this change. But near the end of the eighteenth century, they were still knotting their lines at intervals of forty-eight feet, not the 50⅔ feet needed. In this way they slightly overestimated their speed.

Telescope. With the development of the achromatic lens, telescopes became standard equipment for mariners in the eighteenth century and were soon considered essential for navigation at sea. The reflecting telescope, a small instrument with internal mirrors to help create high magnification, had been commercially available since 1724. However, the typical telescope, made with a nest of cardboard sliding tubes, deteriorated quickly in the dampness on board ships. Seamen preferred to use a spyglass or marine telescope, often made of brass and kept in a protective mahogany case.

Chronometer. As early as 1530, a Flemish professor, Gemma Frisius, observed that if a traveler had an accurate timepiece and compared it with the local time, he could determine differences in longitude. Since a difference of only four minutes in time would account for one degree in longitude, a very accurate clock was needed. In that era only pendulum clocks were accurate enough, but they could not be used in a moving ship. Several countries offered rewards to solve this problem: Spain in 1567 and 1598, the Netherlands about 1600, and England in 1714. Many alternative methods of determining longitude were proposed, including observing lunar distance (between the moon and a fixed star).

Finally, in 1735, Englishman John Harrison made the first clock that could operate accurately in a moving ship. On his second voyage, Captain Cook carried an improved version made by London clockmaker Larcum Kendall. It was a success. With it a navigator could avoid the long calculations needed to determine lunar distances. As Aubrey would later put it in *The Surgeon's Mate*, "Oh, the lunarians may say what they please, but a well-tempered chronometer is the sweetest thing!"

In France, the family firms of Julien and Pierre Le Roy and Ferdinand and Louis Berthoud made fine chronometers. The Berthouds' chronometers were tested at sea for more than a year in two frigates of the French navy and never erred more than half a degree in longitude. French clockmakers like Abraham Bréguet and his son Louis, whose Bréguet timepiece is mentioned in O'Brian's *The Surgeon's Mate*, excelled in quality.

❋

Clearly Aubrey is a cut above the ordinary mariner as he navigates across the high seas and finds the harbors he seeks. His knowledge of mathematics, astronomy, and navigational science, his long apprenticeship charting coasts with ships' masters, and his natural curiosity make him an exceptional pathfinder. His thorough understanding of the winds and the nature of his ship allows him to "crack on" like only a master mariner can. When Aubrey tells his shipmates "there is no time to lose," it carries an added moral authority and presages the complete application of his cunning—and true action.

Aubrey knows that navigating the high seas is a far cry from a simple walk through the streets of Dublin, and in fact Maturin—who places his total faith in Aubrey's skills and nautical intuition—knows it too. Sailing is Aubrey's passion, one that requires his constant vigilance.

Maps of England, Ireland, and Europe

The six maps in this section—England, Southern England, London, Whitehall, Ireland, and Europe—are intended to be a general reference for all seventeen of the Aubrey-Maturin books.

On the map of Southern England, you will find in Sussex the approximate locations of the fictional Melbury Lodge (Aubrey and Maturin's leased bachelor estate), Mapes Court (the Williams's abode), and Grope (one of the homes of Admiral Haddock). In Hampshire, just north of Portsmouth, is Jack and Sophia Aubrey's Ashgrove Cottage (for description, see page 82), and in Dorset are the approximate locations of Woolhampton and Woolcombe House (description, page 149), the latter being the home of General Aubrey. Shelmerston (description, page 148), the home port of the *Surprise* in later books and "the nearest thing to a Caribbean pirates' base that any English country gentlewoman was likely to see," is most likely located on the coast of Devon. A smuggling base and shifty by nature, it seems to rove a bit.

Regarding the locations of Shelmerston and all of the other fictional places that are marked on these maps, the author confesses that he was privy to no more information about their locations than could be found by thoroughly scouring the novels and observing the highly detailed Ordnance Survey maps of England. He apologizes in advance for any deviation from Mr. O'Brian's intended locales but hopes that these approximate placements will help readers to better visualize Aubrey and Maturin's activities in Southern England.

But based on the available clues, I have placed the east-facing town, along with Allacombe (from Shelmerston, the next cove south but one) and Flicken (south by east of Shelmerston) on Torbay, in the vicinity of Paignton, where Patrick O'Brian once attended prep school.

ENGLAND AND WALES

The Spring 1816 volume of *The Naval Chronicle* included the following description of Britain:

> The island of Great Britain is calculated (following its indentations) to have 800 leagues of coast, and presents a very irregular outline, from its numerous gulfs, bays, and estuaries. As a general feature it may be observed that the western coasts are elevated, rising in some places to alpine heights, and warning the navigator of his approach at many leagues distance, while the face of the land declines to the east, and from the North Foreland to Duncan's Bay Head presents a comparatively level and low line, visible but at the distance of a few leagues, or even miles. The south coast is also generally little elevated.
>
> The idea that Great Britain was anciently joined to the Continent has been adopted by many writers, and is principally founded on the similiarity of the strata that compose the cliffs of Dover and Calais, which are alike composed of chalk and flints, and their length on both coasts the same, that is six miles. A narrow ridge of sand and stones, ten miles long, called the Rip-raps, extends between Folkstone and Boulogne, at the distance of ten miles from the former, over which there is but 14 feet water at low spring tides; and another bank, called the Varne, with the same depth, lies about six miles from Dover.
>
> The English Channel, La Manche of the French (Oceanus Britannicus), is 276 miles in length from the Strait of Dover to the Land's End, and its breadth between this latter point and Ushant (Ouessant), called by seamen the "Chops" of the Channel, is 100 miles. In general this gulf, or internal sea, is without shoals or dangers, except near the shores. The depth in mid-channel, from the Land's End to Dengeness, is from 56 to 18 fathoms.
>
> The Strait of Dover (Pas de Calais of the French) is *where* the Channel is the narrowest—between Dover and Cape Griz Nez, 18½ miles, and ... between Dover and Calais piers, 23 miles. The depth in the middle of the Strait is 24 to 18 fathoms. (p. 497)

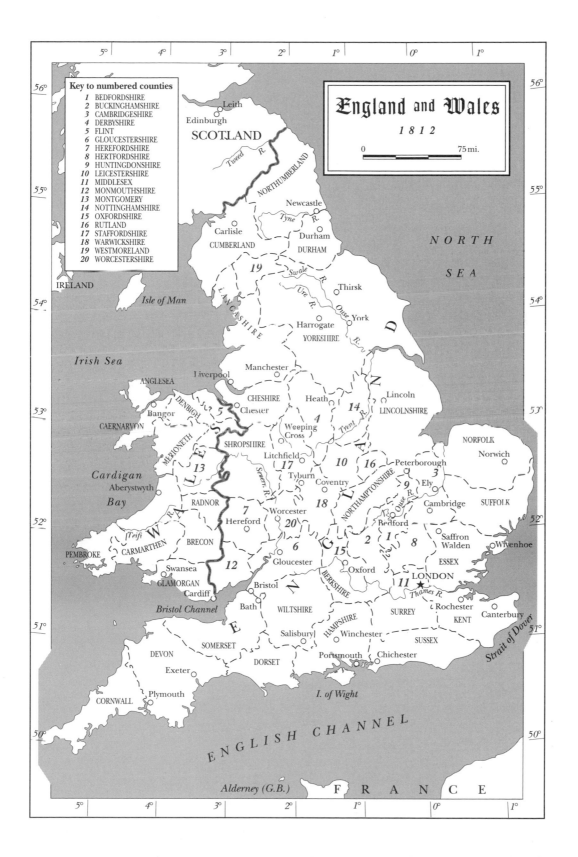

Key to numbered counties

1 BEDFORDSHIRE
2 BUCKINGHAMSHIRE
3 CAMBRIDGESHIRE
4 DERBYSHIRE
5 FLINT
6 GLOUCESTERSHIRE
7 HEREFORDSHIRE
8 HERTFORDSHIRE
9 HUNTINGDONSHIRE
10 LEICESTERSHIRE
11 MIDDLESEX
12 MONMOUTHSHIRE
13 MONTGOMERY
14 NOTTINGHAMSHIRE
15 OXFORDSHIRE
16 RUTLAND
17 STAFFORDSHIRE
18 WARWICKSHIRE
19 WESTMORELAND
20 WORCESTERSHIRE

England and Wales
1812

0   75 mi.

SCOTLAND

IRELAND

NORTH SEA

Leith
Edinburgh

Tweed R.
NORTHUMBERLAND
Newcastle
Tyne R.
Carlisle
Durham
CUMBERLAND
DURHAM

19
Swale R.
Thirsk
Ure R.
Ouse R.
York
Harrogate
YORKSHIRE

Isle of Man

Irish Sea

LANCASHIRE

Liverpool
Manchester
CHESHIRE
Heath
Chester
4
NOTTINGHAMSHIRE
14
Trent R.
Lincoln
LINCOLNSHIRE

ANGLESEA
DENBIGH
Bangor
5
CAERNARVON

Weeping Cross

NORFOLK
Norwich

MERIONETH
SHROPSHIRE
13
Litchfield
17
Tyburn
10
16
Peterborough
3
Ely
SUFFOLK

Cardigan Bay
Aberystwyth
RADNOR
7
Worcester
18
NORTHAMPTONSHIRE
9
Coventry
Ouse R.
Cambridge

Teifi
W
A
L
E
S
BRECON
20
6
15
2
1
Bedford
8
Saffron Walden
Wivenhoe

PEMBROKE
CARMARTHEN
12
Gloucester
Oxford
ESSEX

Swansea
GLAMORGAN
Cardiff
Bristol
11
LONDON
Thames R.
Rochester
Canterbury
KENT

Bristol Channel
Bath
WILTSHIRE
BERKSHIRE
SURREY
Strait of Dover

SOMERSET
Salisbury
HAMPSHIRE
Winchester
SUSSEX
Chichester

DEVON
DORSET
Portsmouth

Exeter
CORNWALL
Plymouth
I. of Wight

ENGLAND

ENGLISH CHANNEL

Alderney (G.B.)
FRANCE

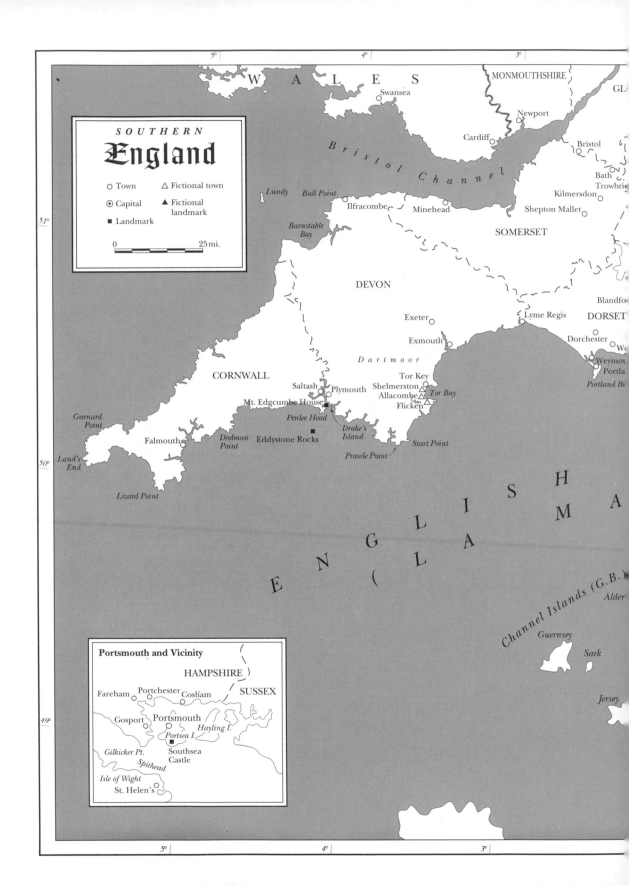

SOUTHERN
England

○ Town   △ Fictional town

◉ Capital   ▲ Fictional landmark

■ Landmark

0   25 mi.

W A L E S

MONMOUTHSHIRE

GL

Swansea

Newport

Cardiff

Bristol

Bath

Trowbri

Kilmersdon

Bristol Channel

Shepton Mallet

Lundy   *Bull Point*

Ilfracombe

Minehead

SOMERSET

Barnstable Bay

DEVON

Blandfo

DORSET

Exeter

Lyme Regis

Dorchester

W

Dartmoor

Exmouth

Weymou

Portla

Portland Bi

CORNWALL

Tor Key

Saltash

Shelmerston △

Plymouth

Allacombe △   *Tor Bay*

Mt. Edgcumbe House ■

Flicken △

Penlee Head

Gurnard Point

Dodman Point

Eddystone Rocks ■

Drake's Island

Falmouth

Start Point

Land's End

Prawle Point

Lizard Point

E N G L I S H   M A

L A

(L

E N

Channel Islands (G.B.)

Alder

Guernsey

Sark

Jersey

Portsmouth and Vicinity

HAMPSHIRE

Fareham

Portchester

Cosham

SUSSEX

Gosport

Portsmouth

Hayling I.

Portsea I.

Gilkicker Pt.

Southsea Castle ■

Spithead

Isle of Wight

St. Helen's

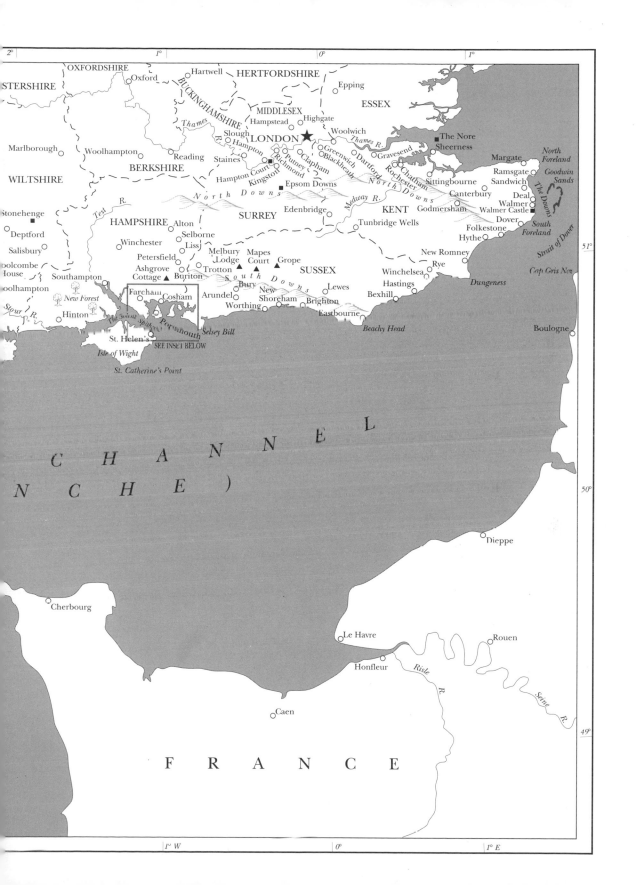

OXFORDSHIRE
Hartwell
HERTFORDSHIRE
Oxford
BUCKINGHAMSHIRE
Epping
ESSEX
MIDDLESEX
Hampstead
Highgate
Woolwich
Slough
LONDON ★
Thames R.
Greenwich
Hampton
Putney
Clapham
Blackheath
The Nore
Sheerness
Marlborough
Woolhampton
Reading
Staines
Richmond
Dartford
Gravesend
Rochester
Chatham
North Foreland
Margate
Ramsgate
North Downs
BERKSHIRE
Hampton Court
Kingston
Epsom Downs
Sittingbourne
Canterbury
Sandwich
Goodwin Sands
WILTSHIRE
Test R.
North Downs
Edenbridge
Medway R.
KENT
Godmersham
Deal
Walmer
Walmer Castle
The Downs
Stonehenge
HAMPSHIRE
Alton
SURREY
Tunbridge Wells
Dover
Deptford
Selborne
Winchester
Liss
South Foreland
Salisbury
Petersfield
Melbury Lodge
Mapes Court
Grope
New Romney
Folkestone
Strait of Dover
51°
oolcombe House
Ashgrove Cottage
Trotton
Buriton
South Downs
Bury
SUSSEX
Rye
Hythe
oolhampton
Southampton
New Forest
Fareham
Cosham
Arundel
New Shoreham
Lewes
Winchelsea
Hastings
Dungeness
Cap Gris Nez
Stour R.
Hinton
The Solent
Spithead
Portsmouth
Selsey Bill
Worthing
Brighton
Bexhill
Eastbourne
Boulogne
St. Helen's
SEE INSET BELOW
Beachy Head
Isle of Wight
St. Catherine's Point

C H A N N E L

(N C H E)

50°

Dieppe

Cherbourg

Le Havre
Rouen

Honfleur
Risle R.
Seine R.

Caen
49°

F R A N C E

SOUTHERN ENGLAND

Maritime activity in southern England began in pre-Roman days, but it received a great boost in the Middle Ages with the creation of the Cinque Ports, a group of port towns that received special privileges from the English Crown in return for providing ships and seamen to guard the Channel and to carry the king's army. As the name (French for "Five Ports") suggests, there were originally five towns—Dover, Hastings, Hythe, Romney, and Sandwich—but Rye, Winchelsea, and others were added later. In the fourteenth century the ports' importance began to decline, largely because their rivers and harbors had become silted up. By the time of the Spanish Armada at the end of the sixteenth century, other southern ports—notably Portsmouth, where the first dry-dock had been built in 1496, and Plymouth—had become important.

IRELAND

Ireland is a detached fragment of the European mainland, separated from the continent by shallow seas. The island is low-lying—most of it is less than five hundred feet above sea level—with an irregular coastline and many natural harbors.

For more than five thousand years, successive waves of settlers arrived on the Emerald Isle from Britain or the Continent. The Vikings founded Dublin, Limerick, and Waterford as trading stations. The influence of the Celts, who came to be known as Gaels, was dominant throughout Ireland but especially along the western coast. The Anglo-Normans invaded in 1170 and established English rule over Dublin and its immediate hinterland (later known as the Pale). In 1641 Oliver Cromwell subdued all of Ireland.

The Society of United Irishmen, formed after the success of the French Revolution, rose up against the British in 1798. The rebellion was quickly snuffed, but it led to passage in 1800 of the Act of Union, which provided for a single parliament for all of the British Isles.

LONDON

London was founded as the Roman town of Londinium in A.D. 43 and—with its location on the River Thames, forty miles from its estuary on the North Sea—became a

Ireland
1812

0   30mi.

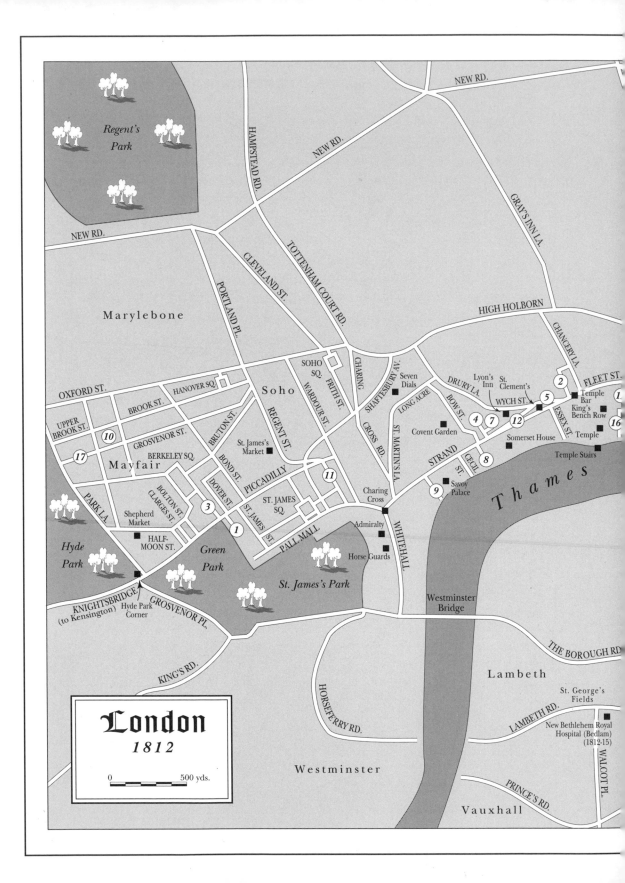

London

1812

0   500 yds.

NEW RD.

Regent's Park

HAMPSTEAD RD.

NEW RD.

NEW RD.

GRAY'S INN LA.

CLEVELAND ST.

TOTTENHAM COURT RD.

PORTLAND PL.

Marylebone

HIGH HOLBORN

CHANCERY LA.

FLEET ST.

OXFORD ST.

HANOVER SQ.

SOHO SQ.

Soho

FRITH ST.

WARDOUR ST.

CHARING

SHAFTESBURY AV.

Seven Dials

Lyon's Inn

St. Clement's

Temple Bar

1

BROOK ST.

REGENT ST.

LONG ACRE

DRURY LA.

WYCH ST.

5

2

King's Bench Row

UPPER BROOK ST.

GROSVENOR ST.

BRUTON ST.

BOW ST.

4 7

12

ESSEX ST.

Temple

10

St. James's Market

ST. MARTIN'S LA.

Covent Garden

Somerset House

16

BERKELEY SQ.

Mayfair

17

BOND ST.

PICCADILLY

CROSS RD.

8

STRAND

CECIL ST.

Temple Stairs

DOVER ST.

ST. JAMES ST.

11

9 Savoy Palace

Thames

PARK LA.

BOLTON ST.
CLARGES ST.

ST. JAMES SQ.

3

Charing Cross

WHITEHALL

Shepherd Market

1

HALF-MOON ST.

PALL MALL

Admiralty

Green Park

Horse Guards

Hyde Park

Westminster Bridge

KNIGHTSBRIDGE
(to Kensington)

Hyde Park Corner

GROSVENOR PL.

St. James's Park

THE BOROUGH RD.

KING'S RD.

Lambeth

St. George's Fields

HORSEFERRY RD.

LAMBETH RD.

New Bethlehem Royal Hospital (Bedlam) (1812-15)

WALCOT PL.

Westminster

PRINCE'S RD.

Vauxhall

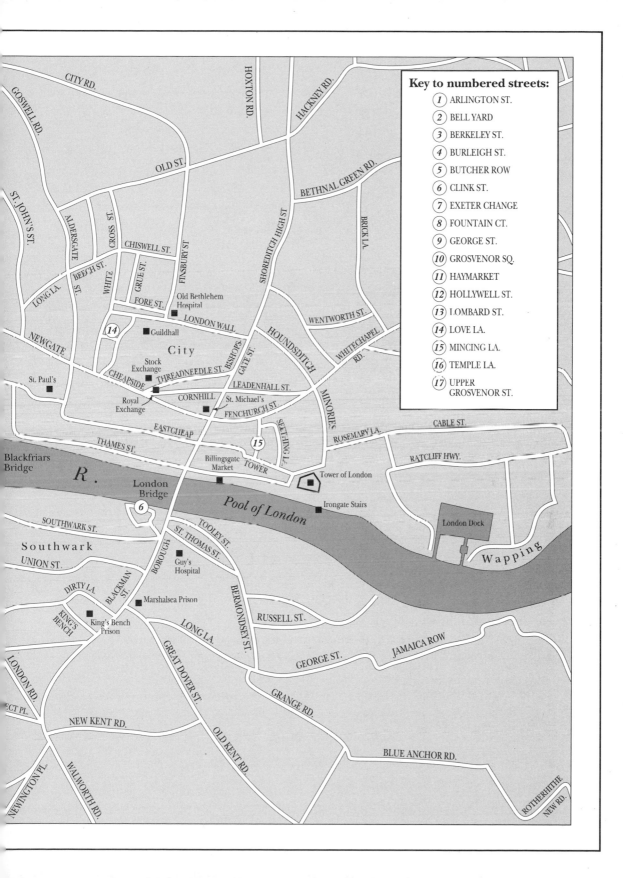

Key to numbered streets:

1. ARLINGTON ST.
2. BELL YARD
3. BERKELEY ST.
4. BURLEIGH ST.
5. BUTCHER ROW
6. CLINK ST.
7. EXETER CHANGE
8. FOUNTAIN CT.
9. GEORGE ST.
10. GROSVENOR SQ.
11. HAYMARKET
12. HOLLYWELL ST.
13. LOMBARD ST.
14. LOVE LA.
15. MINCING LA.
16. TEMPLE LA.
17. UPPER GROSVENOR ST.

prosperous trading center in Anglo-Saxon times. In 1066, after the Normans invaded Britain, William the Conqueror granted London its charter and made the city his capital.

Throughout the Middle Ages the city was the center of government, commerce, and trade for England. In the seventeenth century London was hit by the Great Plague, which took the lives of 100,000 people, and a fire that destroyed a large portion of the city. The city was rebuilt—largely according to the designs of the architect Sir Christopher Wren—and became the most important trading center in the world during the eighteenth century.

One of London's oldest landmarks is the Tower of London, an ancient building complex on the north bank of the Thames. The first stone section—the White Tower—was begun by William the Conqueror in 1078. The complex consists of concentric fortifications, moats, bastions, and thirteen towers. A royal residence until the early seventeenth century, the Tower has also served as a prison, an armory, and a storehouse for royal treasure. To the west of the Tower lies the City, the one-mile-square heart of London and the site of the Royal Exchange, the Stock Exchange, and Wren's seventeenth-century Saint Paul's Cathedral. The oldest bridge spanning the Thames—in fact, the only one until Westminster Bridge was built in 1749—is London Bridge. The original wooden bridge was built by the Romans, and the first stone structure was constructed between 1176 and 1209.

WHITEHALL

In the district of Westminster, Whitehall houses the chief government buildings, including the Admiralty, the Treasury, the prime minister's residence at 10 Downing Street, and the Horse Guards (headquarters of the army). The site was originally the location of the huge, rambling Whitehall Palace, which in 1532 became Henry VIII's premier royal residence in London. The palace expanded over the years until 1698, when a fire destroyed everything but the Renaissance-style Banqueting House, designed by the architect Inigo Jones in 1619.

The Admiralty is a brick building with a large Ionic portico built between 1722 and 1726. In 1761 a screen with winged sea horses surmounting the gates was added.

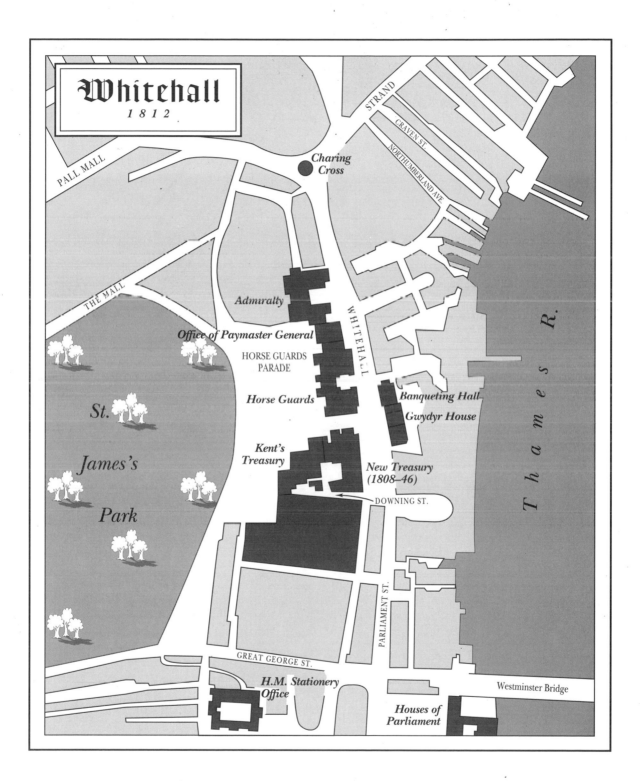

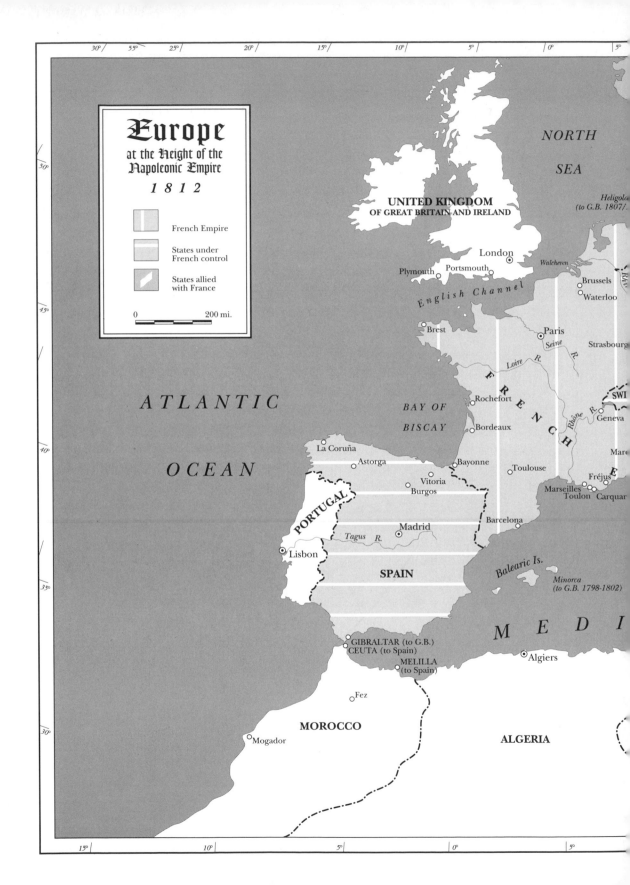

30° 55° 25° 20° 15° 10° 5° 0° 5°

NORTH

SEA

Heligola
(to G.B. 1807/

UNITED KINGDOM
OF GREAT BRITAIN AND IRELAND

London ⊙

Walcheren

Bay

Brussels ○
Waterloo ○

Plymouth ○ Portsmouth ○

English Channel

Brest ○

Paris ⊙
Seine R.

Strasbourg

Loire R.

F R E N C H

Rochefort ○

SWI

Rhône R.

Geneva ○

ATLANTIC

BAY OF

BISCAY

Bordeaux ○

Mars

OCEAN

La Coruña ○

Astorga ○

Bayonne ○

Toulouse ○

Fréjus ○

Marseilles ○
Toulon ○ Carquar

Vitoria ○
Burgos ○

E

PORTUGAL

Madrid ⊙

Barcelona ○

Tagus R.

Balearic Is.

Lisbon ⊙

SPAIN

Minorca
(to G.B. 1798-1802)

M E D I

GIBRALTAR (to G.B.) ○
CEUTA (to Spain) ○
MELILLA ○
(to Spain)

Algiers ⊙

Fez ○

MOROCCO

ALGERIA

Mogador ○

15° 10° 5° 0° 5°

Map legend:

Europe

at the Height of the
Napoleonic Empire

1 8 1 2

French Empire

States under
French control

States allied
with France

0   200 mi.

DENMARK AND NORWAY

SWEDEN

Stockholm

BALTIC SEA

penhagen

Hamburg
MECKLENBURG

ESTPHALIA
unswick

Berlin

Leipzig

SAXONY

Jena

Dresden

FEDERATION

THE RHINE

BERG

PRUSSIA

Danzig

Tilsit

Friedland

Warsaw

WARSAW

Oder R.

Vistula R.

Niemen R.

Borisov

Berezina R.

Pripet R.

Kiev

Dnieper R.

Bug R.

RUSSIAN
EMPIRE

Moscow

Borodino

Ulm

BAVARIA

Saale R.

TYROL

ITALY

San Marino

Danube R.

Vienna

Buda

Pest

Drave R.

Save R.

ILLYRIAN PROVINCES

Austerlitz

Wagram

AUSTRIAN

EMPIRE

Dniester R.

Prut R.

Danube R.

Sea of
Azov

BLACK SEA

an
R.

noa

SAN
MARINO

R
E

Elba

io
rsica

Rome

Naples

NAPLES

SARDINIA

liari

ADRIATIC SEA

MONTENEGRO

Cattaro

OTTOMAN

Constantinople

EMPIRE

Corfu
(to Fr. 1807-14)

Ionian Is.
(Russ. Prot. to 1807;
to Fr. 1807-1809;
to G.B. 1809-1815;
thereafter G.B. Prot.)

AEGEAN SEA

Rhodes

Cyprus

Palermo

SICILY

Malta (to Fr. 1798-99;
to G.B. 1800-1814)

Crete

Alexandria

Port Said

TERRANEAN SEA

JNIS

TRIPOLI

EGYPT

Nile

10°   15°   20°   25°   30°   35°   40°   45°   55°

50°

45°

40°

35°

30°

10°   15°   20°   25°   30°   35°

EUROPE

In 1812 much of Europe was in Napoleon's hands. Germany and Austria had fallen in 1805. Both Prussia and Russia were forced to make peace with France in 1807. The following year Napoleon installed his brother as king of Spain and also seized Portugal. In April 1809 the Austrians launched the War of the Fifth Coalition with France, but they were crushed a few months later.

By 1810 the British were able to expel the French from Portugal, and in July 1812 they defeated the French army in Spain. In June of that year Napoleon invaded Russia with forces numbering more than 450,000, reaching Moscow by September, before the bitter cold and the overwhelming Russian forces forced him to retreat with the bedraggled remnants of his army. After Napoleon's debacle in Russia, the Prussians deserted their alliance with the French.

THE NOVELS

Key to Maps
in Chapters 1 to 17

In the following chapters, most of the voyages taken in the Aubrey-Maturin novels are mapped out. The key below applies to all of these route maps.

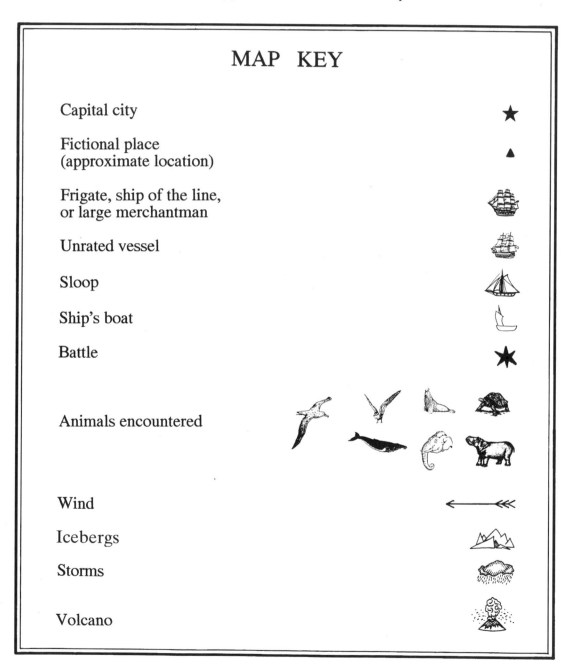

MAP KEY

Capital city	★
Fictional place (approximate location)	▲
Frigate, ship of the line, or large merchantman	
Unrated vessel	
Sloop	
Ship's boat	
Battle	✶
Animals encountered	
Wind	←—««
Icebergs	
Storms	
Volcano	

Mastering
the Mediterranean

As Patrick O'Brian readily confesses, he modeled many of the events of the novel *Master and Commander* on the remarkable Mediterranean cruise of Lord Cochrane (later, tenth earl of Dundonald) aboard the *Speedy*, a dwarfish brig that Cochrane once called "little more than a burlesque on a vessel of war." Consider Cochrane's account of his assignment to the *Speedy:* "The vessel originally intended for me by Lord Keith was the *Bonne Citoyenne*, a fine corvette of eighteen guns, but the brother of his lordship's secretary happening at the time to arrive from Gibraltar ... that functionary managed to place his brother in one of the finest sloops in the service, leaving to me the least efficient craft on the station." The similarity of this true event to the circumstances surrounding Aubrey's appointment to the *Sophie* in *Master and Commander* is no mistake.

Like the *Speedy*, the *Sophie* must return a pair of 12-pounders to the ordnance wharf because her timbers cannot bear the concussion, and she too can carry only ten tons of water. Both brigs ship the fore-topgallant yard of the *Généreaux* as a main yard and plane the yardarms to fool port officials. And like the *Speedy*, the pint-size *Sophie*, a mouse among elephants, begins her cruise at Port Mahon, on the island of Minorca, and goes on to wreak havoc in the western Mediterranean.

In 1800 Port Mahon is a town bustling with war. It is a place where men and women of varied backgrounds and allegiances have been thrust together. The stamp of England, nonetheless, has been firmly imprinted on the port, since the British have occupied Minorca throughout much of the eighteenth century. In fact, the hotel where

Aubrey stays was built in 1750, when the British controlled the island, and is named after The Crown, an inn in Portsmouth.

It is in Port Mahon that Aubrey and Maturin meet. Their mutual love of music brings them together and, despite their very different natures, they do have more than a little in common: both are broke, both are out of work, and both are in need of an opportunity. It comes on April 1, 1800, when Aubrey is made captain of the *Sophie* and then induces Maturin to ship as his surgeon.

At first assigned the lowly duty of convoying merchant ships, the *Sophie* sails east from Minorca along the 39th parallel with a dozen merchant ships to Cagliari, a fortified seaport on the southern coast of Sardinia. From Cagliari she escorts another convoy of merchant ships north to Leghorn (Livorno), a major Tuscan seaport, which is neutral and open to ships of all nations. In the Genoa roads, Aubrey gets his break when Lord Keith, Admiral of the Blue and commander in chief in the Mediterranean, orders the *Sophie* to cruise the French and Spanish coasts down to Cape Nao to menace their commercial ports and vessels. In short order Aubrey, like Cochrane, takes full advantage of this command and makes his overachieving ship an infamous nuisance to the enemy.

Spanish merchants convince their government to send the 32-gun xebec-frigate *Cacafuego* after Aubrey. But he, like Cochrane, fools the bigger ship by pretending to be a Danish brig with a plague-ridden crew. In both instances the deception is so successful that the smaller ship might have seized the opportunity to attack her predator, but in both the captain refuses to take this perhaps morally unfair advantage, raising eyebrows as to his courage among his less conscientious crew.

Following a return to Port Mahon and an errand to Sir Sydney Smith's squadron off Alexandria, Egypt, the *Sophie* sails back to Minorca and then is allowed another cruise. She sails to Barcelona, Spain, once again playing cat and mouse with the merchant vessels on the busy Spanish coast, even brazenly taunting the gunboats protecting the Barcelona harbor. Early one morning the *Sophie* sails past the mouth of the Llobregat River, which flows southeast from the Pyrenees Mountains and enters the sea three miles south of Barcelona, when she again meets the *Cacafuego*.

Following an all-too-brief refit in Port Mahon, the *Sophie* is ordered away again, this time for Malta, to be refitted more fully, and then, regrettably, to Gibraltar with the mail. In his anger at having the *Sophie*'s cruise cut short and for other abuses from Admiral Harte at Port Mahon, Aubrey gives this assignment a rather liberal interpretation. A nighttime shore attack against three Spanish coasting vessels off the coast of Spain results in an encounter with a formidable French squadron—including the ships *Formidable, Indomptable, Desaix,* and *Muiron*—under Rear Admiral Linois.

At the conclusion of *Master and Commander,* Aubrey witnesses two great battles from different sides of Bay Algeciras. In the first—when an English squadron under the nonfictional Admiral James Saumarez sails into the bay and attacks the French squadron and batteries—Aubrey views the encounter from a somewhat disadvantageous point of view on the west side of the bay—that is to say, in Algeciras. With Maturin, Aubrey watches the second action, which occurs in the Strait of Gibraltar, from the eastern side of the bay, high atop the Rock of Gibraltar.

HERE AND THERE

Algeciras Bay
Also called the Bay of Gibraltar, a body of water at the eastern end of the Strait of Gibraltar that separates the Spanish-controlled seaport of Algeciras from the British-held Gibraltar by just six miles.

Gibraltar
A peninsula on the southern coast of Spain at the western end of the Mediterranean Sea, notable for its strategic rocky promontory, fourteen hundred feet high. Encompassing only about two and a quarter square miles, Gibraltar is, nonetheless, an ideal location for controlling the Strait of Gibraltar, the passage between the Mediterranean and the Atlantic Ocean. Still, the occupation of Gibraltar was a costly prospect both financially and in terms of relations with Spain. As Vice Admiral Sir George Collier once declared in the House of Commons: "I have long looked upon Gibraltar as a military millstone about the neck of this country. . . . Sir, I suppose, if the many millions Gibraltar has cost Great Britain since it has been in our possession were to be changed into silver, it would go near to encrustate the whole rock" (*The Naval Chronicle*, Fall 1814, p. 400). During the Napoleonic wars, some favored relinquishing control of Gibraltar and maintaining a similar strategic presence by annexing Ceuta on the Barbary Coast.

Captured by Britain and her allies in 1704 during the War of the Spanish Succession, Gibraltar was made a British colony by the Treaty of Utrecht in 1713. During the American Revolution, it was continually under siege from the French and the Spanish.

NEXT PAGE: Cruising the western Mediterranean in the *Sophie*, Captain Aubrey faces off against a number of enemy merchants and men-of-war and earns the nickname "Lucky Jack," not to mention a pretty penny in prizes.

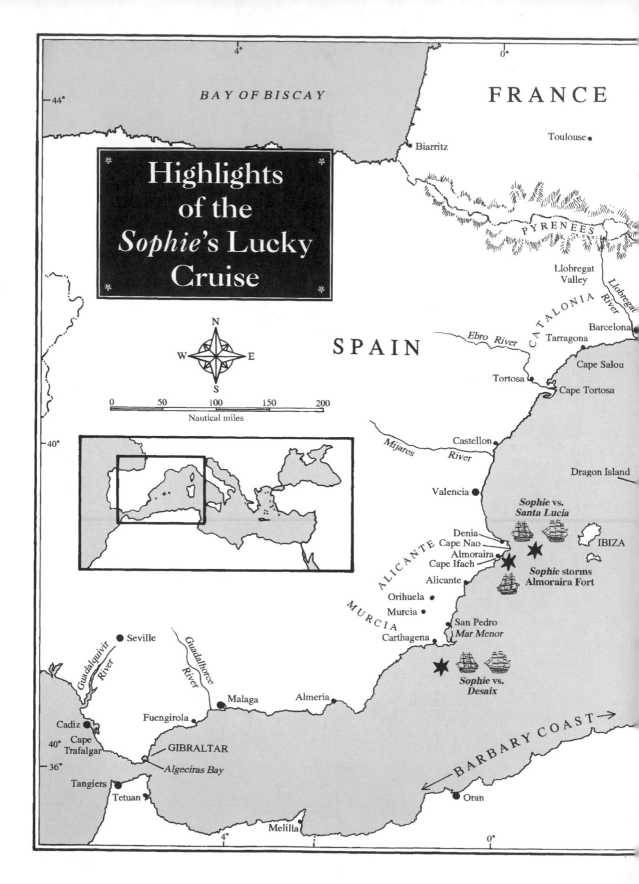

BAY OF BISCAY

FRANCE

• Biarritz

Toulouse •

PYRENEES

Highlights of the *Sophie*'s Lucky Cruise

Llobregat Valley

CATALONIA

Llobregat River

SPAIN

Ebro River

Tarragona

Barcelona

Cape Salou

Tortosa •

Cape Tortosa

N
W — E
S

0   50   100   150   200
Nautical miles

Mijares River

Castellon •

Dragon Island

Valencia •

Sophie vs. *Santa Lucia*

Denia
Cape Nao
Almoraira
Cape Ifach

IBIZA

ALICANTE

Alicante •

Sophie storms Almoraira Fort

Orihuela •
Murcia •

MURCIA

San Pedro
Mar Menor

Carthagena •

Guadalquivir River

Seville •

Guadalhorce River

Malaga •

Almeria •

Sophie vs. *Desaix*

BARBARY COAST →

Cadiz •
Cape Trafalgar
40°
GIBRALTAR
36°
Algeciras Bay

Fuengirola •

Tangiers •
Tetuan •

← Oran •

Melilla •

4°

Rhône River

mistral

LANGUEDOC

PROVENCE

mistral

8°

44°

Genoa

Nice

Cannes

Sophie

Leghorn
(Livorno)

Agde
Cette
arbonne

Marseilles
Toulon

Hyères

mistral

Hyères I.
Giens
Gulf of Giens
Cape Sicie

tramontana

Elba I.

Monte Cristo

Port-
endes

★
Sophie vs.
L'Aimable Louise

GULF OF LIONS

Cape Creus

CORSICA

Ajaccio

Palafrugell
Palamos

★
Sophie vs.
Cacafuego

Pt.
Fornells

Ciudadela
C. Dartuch

C. Mola
Mt. Toro
Port
Mahon
Ayrc
Island

SARDINIA

40°

MAJORCA

MINORCA

MINORCA
0   10   20   30
Nautical miles

Cagliari

Cape Teulada

MEDITERRANEAN   SEA

Cape
Bourgaroun

Algiers

A L G E R I A

T U N I S

36°

4°

8°

Minorca

One of the Balearic Islands, in the western Mediterranean off the coast of Spain. The Balearics—comprising the four main islands of Ibiza, Majorca, Minorca, and Formentera, and numerous smaller islands—are actually partially submerged peaks that are a continuation of the mountains of southeastern Spain.

For the English, Minorca offers some of the comforts of home but better weather. "In rough weather the spray of the sea is driven over the whole island," reports the fall edition of the 1799 *Naval Chronicle*. "The air . . . is much more clear and pure than in Britain" (p. 125). A low-lying island, Minorca's rough, uneven topography is rilled by deep, narrow valleys, known locally as *barancoes*, that emanate from the island's interior and stretch down to the sea.

The same edition of *The Naval Chronicle* sketches the island's complicated history:

> Minorca first fell under the power of the Romans, afterwards of the northern Barbarians; from them it was taken by the Arabs, who were subdued by the king of Majorca, who surrendered it to the King of Spain. The English subdued it in 1708, under General Stanhope; it came under the government of the French in June 1756; was restored to this country by the treaty of Paris in 1763; surrendered to the Duc de Crillon, Commander in Chief of the combined armies of France and Spain, on the 5th of February 1782; and again came into the possession of the English on the 15th of November 1798, when attacked by the squadron under Commodore Duckworth, with troops commanded by the Honourable General Charles Stuart. (p. 125)

The Spanish regained Minorca in 1802 by the Treaty of Amiens, but the British continued to use the island during the Napoleonic wars.

Port Mahon

The chief town and port of Minorca, located on the island's southeastern coast. Port Mahon is not only strategically located (225 miles south of Toulon, 100 miles southeast of Barcelona, and 150 miles north of the main sea route between Gibraltar and Naples), but it also has one of the finest natural harbors in the Mediterranean. Indeed, a popular old saying proclaims, "The Mediterranean has three good harbors: June, July, and Port Mahon." The harbor's entrance was guarded by the powerful fortress of St. Philip. The town sits at the back of the harbor, some three miles from the fort.

Mahon Harbor. The anxiety with which the public mind is at present directed towards the Mediterranean made us wish to gratify our readers with a correct view of this commodious and excellent harbor, which is now, when most wanted, in our possession. The design was made by Mr. Pocock from a most accurate drawing done at Mahon (usually pronounced Ma-on) in 1773 for the late General James Johnstone, then Governor.

This view of the harbor was taken from the north, opposite to Cale Figuiere. Among other things depicted here are the church and convent des Carmes, the Bureau de la Santé, the Port of Mahon, the magazine for victualling the Navy, the Admiral's house, the parish church, the convent, the town clock, the place to careen the ships, the Governor's house, and the Church of St. François.

Mahon harbor is full of little coves, similar to Cale Figuiere, which afford excellent anchorage; as indeed does in general the whole harbor, which is chiefly of an equal depth from shore to shore; the bottom is mostly covered with a thick grass, owing to which a light anchor will not take hold; a good scope of cable is therefore necessary to be given before you check the ship. Mahon harbor, allowed to be the finest in the Mediterranean, is about 90 fathoms wide at its entrance, but within very large and safe, stretching a league or more into the land.

Mahon, which derives its name from Mago, the Carthaginian General who founded the town, stands on an eminence on the west side of the harbor, the ascent pretty steep. It is large, but the streets are winding, narrow, and ill paved. There is a fine wharf at the foot of the hill, on which Mahon stands, the western end of which is set apart for careening and repairing his Majesty's ships. The depth of water is such, that ships of the largest size can come close to the quay. (Fall 1799 edition of *The Naval Chronicle*, p. 125.)

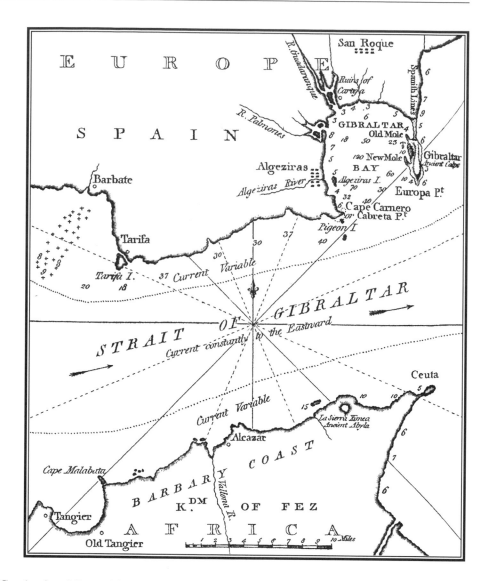

Chart of Strait of and Bay of Gibraltar. Whether Gibraltar, considered in a political light, is regarded as the key to Mediterranean commerce or—impregnable as it has been rendered by art and nature—a post from whence a British armament may issue to the terror of its foes or retire in perfect safety from the insults of a superior enemy, it has certainly become a place of considerable consequence to Britain. Though possessed of no trade or actual commerce that may return the expense of maintaining it, there can be no doubt that, contrary to the opinion of some, the secondary benefits arising from the possession of a post so situated would fully warrant a tenfold expenditure on its support. (Spring 1818 edition of *The Naval Chronicle*, p. 232.)

Strait of Gibraltar (the Gut)

The passage between Spain and Africa that connects the Mediterranean Sea to the Atlantic Ocean. At the western end of the 36-mile strait, Cape Trafalgar stands to the north and Spartel to the south. At the eastern end, Gibraltar stands to the north and Ceuta to the south. The strait is about eight miles wide at its narrowest point and 23 miles wide at its widest. The two promontories at the eastern end of the strait, the Rock of Gibraltar and the Jebel Musa at Ceuta, form the mythical Pillars of Hercules.

England, the Continent, and a North Atlantic Showdown

Having been cleared by court-martial in Gibraltar for losing the *Sophie* at the end of book 1, *Master and Commander*, Aubrey sails as a passenger, with Maturin, for England on board the *Charwell*, a frigate just back from the West Indies. The two find themselves suddenly snatched from the jaws of yet another underdog confrontation with the enemy, this time in the Bay of Biscay off the coast of Brest, and thrust into the uncertainties of peace. The Treaty of Amiens has just been signed in March 1802.

Back in England, Aubrey and Maturin settle into Melbury Lodge on the South Downs in Sussex, fox-hunting country within a day's ride of London. Melbury Lodge is fortuitously within the social sphere of Grope, Admiral Haddock's house, and Mapes Court, home of the Williams family. Melbury is also not far north of Midshipman Babbington's family home in the town of Arundel, a seaport five miles from the mouth of the Arun River, which flows into the Channel at Littlehampton. In Arundel, Aubrey manages to get into a ruckus of a political nature that will hurt him at the Admiralty later. After further embroiling themselves in the foibles of shore life—in this case, primarily debt and female related—Aubrey and Maturin finally make their escape.

They sail to Toulon, a seaport on the southeastern coast of France, where they dine with the French captain Christy-Pallière, whom they had befriended when they were prisoners of his aboard the *Desaix*. While there, Maturin plans to study the flora and fauna of Porquerolles, one of the Hyères Islands off the coast. But in case hostilities with

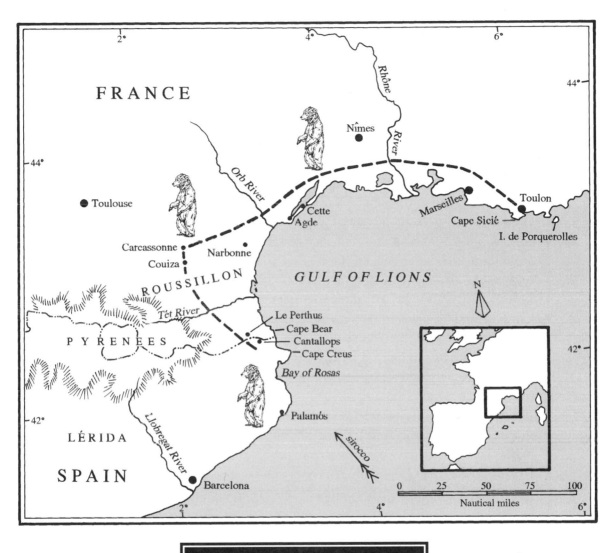

❋ "Can He Dance, Mate?" ❋

Caught in Toulon, France, in 1803 at the start of the Napoleonic War, Aubrey and Maturin don disguises and hike across France to the safety of the Maturin family castle in Catalonia.

France resume, he is also gathering intelligence, particularly about Catalonia and about Port Mahon, Minorca, which had been returned to the Spanish by the Treaty of Amiens.

    War does in fact break out again, and in one of the most outlandish episodes of the Aubrey-Maturin novels, the pair escapes from France by traveling incognito around the

Gulf of Lions and through the Pyrenees. They are headed for Maturin's family home, a somewhat dilapidated old castle in the Pyrenees Mountains behind Figueras, a fortified town in the northeast of Spain that was occupied by the French in 1794, 1808, and 1811. Aubrey barely survives the many rugged days of climbing in the Pyrenees, which reach altitudes of more than eleven thousand feet. Finally, after trudging hundreds of miles, they reach Maturin's castle and take in a vast view of Catalonia, Cape Creus, and the Bay of Rosas along the Mediterranean coast. For details of the route, see the map "Can He Dance, Mate?."

Next, Aubrey and Maturin board Captain Spottiswood's *Lord Nelson*, an East Indiaman bound for England from Gibraltar. The busy Bay of Biscay provides the *Lord Nelson* with an eventful homeward passage—including an encounter with the *Bellone*, a 34-gun Bordeaux privateer—and a not altogether direct path to Plymouth.

Back in London too late for a plum assignment, Aubrey dodges debt collectors and bides his time, taking respite in the Duchy of Lancaster, or the Savoy, where he is safe from tipstaffs. At a party thrown by Lady Keith, he meets a Bristol merchant named Canning and briefly considers taking command of a letter of marque. But when Lord Melville offers him the command of the "experimental vessel" *Polychrest*, he gladly accepts and removes himself immediately to Portsmouth, where she is fitting out.

Having received most of their complement either from prison or from the quotas of Huntingdonshire (a former county now mostly in Cambridgeshire) and Rutland (now part of Leicestershire)—both in central England and able to supply only thorough land-lubbers—Aubrey and Tom Pullings set about revamping the crew of the *Polychrest*. When Pullings's parents come over from near New Forest, a hunting preserve in southwest Hampshire, to throw a feast in honor of his commission as lieutenant, the *Polychrest* adds several uninvited party guests of a thuggish nature to her number.

A cruise in the Channel allows Aubrey to improve the crew and the *Polychrest*'s sailing qualities somewhat. But on her first mission—a rendezvous off Cape Gris Nez, the closest part of the French coast to England, fifteen miles southwest of Calais—it is clear that she remains an unwieldy beast. Her second outing—convoying merchant ships bound for the west coast of Africa as far as Lisbon—is even worse. The under-manned *Polychrest* is slow and clumsy, an embarassment. Left alone at last, Aubrey and his crew rerig the sloop off the coast of Portugal.

Entering the Bay of Biscay from the south, near Cape Ortegal, Spain, the *Polychrest* sights three ships, one of which proves to be Captain Dumanoir's *Bellone*, the Bordeaux privateer that had earlier drubbed the *Lord Nelson* when Aubrey and Maturin were passengers. A bloody battle ensues, carrying the two ships as far east as Gijón, a commercial seaport on the northwest coast of Spain.

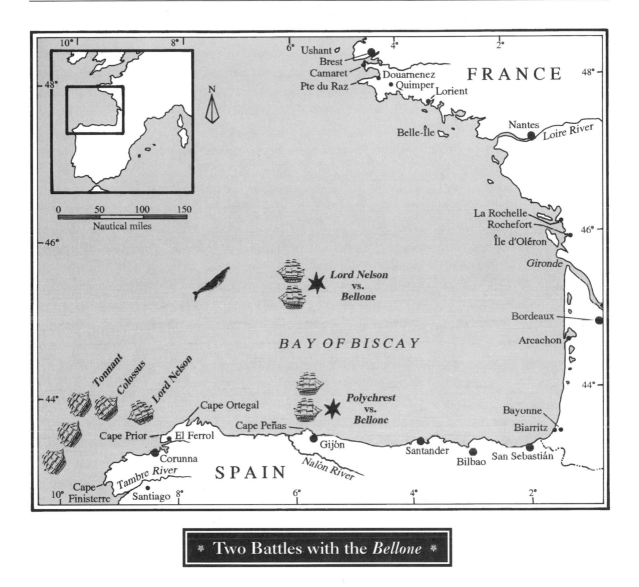

❋ Two Battles with the *Bellone* ❋

First as passenger on board the *Lord Nelson* and later as commander of the *Worcester*, Aubrey battles the Bordeaux privateer *Bellone* in the Bay of Biscay.

After returning to England, the *Polychrest* is sent to the Baltic, while Maturin makes an intelligence foray to Spain via Ireland. He travels through Aragon, an ancient kingdom in northeast Spain that was united with Castile in 1479 after the marriage of Ferdinand and Isabella, and visits Montserrat, a ninth-century monastery and ecclesiastical center in the high Pyrenees near Barcelona.

On the verge of mutual destruction over personal affairs, Aubrey and Maturin are called to duty in the nick of time, albeit to the northeast coast of France in what seems—given the *Polychrest*'s sailing capabilities and the deficiencies of her crew—a suicidal mission, intentionally planned by the malevolent cuckold Admiral Harte. Before he can fight the French, Aubrey also must deal with a mutinous crew that plans to take and carry the *Polychrest* into Saint-Valéry, France.

Back in England, Aubrey is lauded for his action on the French coast and is given a temporary assignment aboard the frigate *Lively,* whose captain is away sitting in Parliament. On the Channel coast of France, Aubrey exercises the *Lively,* a crack sailing ship but an inexperienced fighter, by attacking batteries at Balbec and Barfleur and a semaphore station at Cape Levi. But he cannot avoid some dreary troop-transport duty that begins at Plymouth—within sight of Admiral Haddock's official residence atop Mount Edgcumb—and terminates at the Nore, in the mouth of the Thames.

It is now the autumn of 1804, and Maturin, having provided Whitehall with crucial intelligence regarding Spain's entry into the war, secures Aubrey and the *Lively* a related assignment. No, the *Lively* is not headed for Madeira, the Portuguese island off the Moroccan coast, or for Fernando Poo, in the Bight of Biafra off the west coast of Africa, as the crew nervously speculates when Maturin and a messenger board the *Lively* in the Nore. Even Captain Aubrey—who is told to rendezvous with *Indefatigable, Medusa,* and *Amphion* off Dodman Point, a cape on the south coast of Cornwall—will not know the nature of his mission until he reaches 43 degrees of latitude.

Of course, as Maturin already knows, this newly formed squadron of four English frigates is to intercept four Spanish frigates laden with treasure crucial to Spain's war effort. The Spanish treasure is bound from Montevideo, a South American seaport on the River Plate, to Cadiz, on the south coast of Spain near the Strait of Gibraltar.

HERE AND THERE

Bath

A city in Avon County, England, situated on the steep slopes of the River Avon, twelve miles southeast of Bristol. The Romans used to visit the city for its hot mineral springs, and the baths they built here around A.D. 55—the finest Roman ruins in Britain—were discovered in 1775. Bath came to be a fashionable spa for the gentry under the influence of the famous gambler and socialite Beau Nash, who became the city's master of ceremonies in 1705. Many elegant new buildings were erected in Bath during the eighteenth century. Most notable of these was the Royal Crescent, an arc of Palladian-style row houses designed by John Wood the Younger in the 1760s.

Bay of Biscay

A large inlet of the Atlantic Ocean along the west coast of France and the north coast of Spain. The bay was infamous among sailors for its rough seas and sudden storms.

Cadiz

Spain's principal port for trade with the American colonies, located fifty-eight miles northwest of Gibraltar. The city sits on a narrow, rocky peninsula that forms the protected harbor of the Bay of Cadiz. In 1493 Columbus embarked from Cadiz on his second voyage to the New World. As the headquarters of the Spanish treasure fleets, Cadiz was attacked in 1587 by Sir Francis Drake, who sank, burned, or captured over thirty ships that were preparing to invade England. The British attacked again in 1702 but failed to seize the city. From 1797 to 1798, the port was blockaded by the British, and Nelson bombarded it in 1800. From 1810 to 1812, as the capital of insurgent Spain reinforced by friendly British forces, it was besieged by the French.

Chatham

A town and port on the River Medway in Kent, England, thirty miles southeast of London. An important naval base, Chatham's royal dockyard was established by Henry VIII in the sixteenth century. The defenses east of town erected against a possible invasion by Napoleon between 1803 and 1805 can still be seen today.

The Downs, North and South

Two ranges of low-lying chalk hills extending from west to east across Hampshire and Sussex in southern England. Leith Hill, at 965 feet, is the highest point in the North Downs, and 889-foot Butser Hill is the highest point in the South Downs.

English Channel or the Channel

An arm of the Atlantic Ocean between southern England and northern France. Called La Manche ("The Sleeve") in French, the Channel connects the Atlantic on the west with the North Sea on the east via the Strait of Dover. With its unpredictable, often foggy weather and its strong and unusual tides, the Channel has seen countless shipwrecks over the centuries. For Britain it has served as a barrier to invasion, although it was crossed by Julius Caesar's legions in 55 B.C. and by Norman forces under William the Conqueror in 1066. Napoleon's plans to cross the Channel were never realized.

A map of Cadiz. Until now, the city of Cadiz had never been attacked by a power that did not have a superior naval force. The Island of Leon, on the northwest extremity of which it lies, forms with the opposite shore, a bay about six miles wide. Near the middle of the bay on two points of land; one on the Continent, the other on the island, 500 fathoms asunder, stand the forts Puntal and Matagorda, which command the passage. The latter surrendered to the French on the 21st of last April (1809).

As the French must circle the bay, they will have to march 27 English miles before reaching the Isle of Leon, which, seven miles from Cadiz, is strongly fortified and garrisoned with 10,000 men. The narrow neck of land leading to Cadiz is flanked by the sea on one side and by the bay on the other. Nowhere more than half a mile broad, the isthmus is enfiladed by gunboats and men of war, and protected by *chevaux de frise* [wooden poles with pointed tips used as underwater obstructions to prevent the passage of ships or landing boats]. Supposing the French in possession of the Isle of Leon, they must march on this narrow causeway until they are again opposed by fortifications with about 30 pieces of heavy artillery that completely command the road.

If again successful, the French have a good carriage way until they arrive in front of Cadiz, where the ground is mined for half a mile. They will then encounter between 60 and 70 pieces of cannon on the outer walls, which command the approach to Cadiz. These walls must be regularly attacked, but even supposing them to be forced, there is a second fortification behind them with drawbridges and flanked by the heaviest ordnance. A *coup de main* is out of the question, and because of the open nature of the ground and the loose sandy soil, regular approaches are difficult. It may be added that from the sea the breakers by which Cadiz is nearly surrounded form an important and formidable defense. (Spring 1810 edition of *The Naval Chronicle*, p. 473.)

Goodwin Sands

A treacherous underwater bank of shifting sands at the northern end of the Strait of Dover, about seven miles east of Deal, England. The sands, which form a shelter for the roadstead and anchorage called the Downs (not to be confused with the hills called the North and South Downs), are said to have once been part of an island owned by Earl Godwin that was destroyed by a violent storm in the eleventh century. Many ships have

A view of Walmer Castle. The Village of Walmer—probably, *quasi vallum maris*, that is, the wall, or fortification made against the sea—is situated about a mile to the south of Deal and about half a mile from the seashore. Walmer Castle is one of the three castles (Walmer, Deal, and Sandown) built by King Henry the VIII in 1539 to defend the coast. By Act 32 of the same sovereign, it was placed under the government of the Lord Warden of the Cinque Ports (Chartered by William in 1077 to protect the coast and serve as naval bases, the original Cinque Ports were Hastings, Dover, Hithe, Romney, and Sandwich).

Walmer Castle has four round lunettes of very thick stone arched work and many large portholes. In the middle is a great round tower with a cistern at the top and underneath an arched cavern, bomb proof. The castle, encompassed by a moat crossed by a drawbridge, occupies a remarkably pleasant situation near the shore with an uninterrupted view of the Downs and the Channel as far as the coast of France. The apartments towards the sea, having been modernized, have been used some years by the constable and Lord Warden of Dover Castle, for his residence in that part of the country. The truly great Mr. Pitt, the late Lord Warden, resided there whenever his public duties would permit his absence from the capital. (Spring 1807 edition of *The Naval Chronicle*, p. 50.)

met with disaster on the sands over the centuries despite such warning devices as buoys and lightships.

The Liberties of the Savoy

A liberty was a district within the limits of a county but exempt from the jurisdiction of the sheriff. The Liberties of the Savoy was the property of the English royal house of Lancaster, originally the grounds of John of Gaunt's Savoy Palace, between the City of London and Westminster. Bounded by the Strand to the north, the Thames to the south, Ivy Bridge to the west, and the Temple to the east, the Liberties were, as O'Brian explains in *The Thirteen Gun Salute*, "legally . . . not part of London or Westminster at all, but of the Duchy of Lancaster, and culturally it was a self-contained village."

The Nore

A sandbank and anchorage located in the Thames estuary near the mouth of the River Medway. It was the most heavily used naval and merchant ship anchorage in Britain and a major rendezvous for naval vessels convoying merchant ships. There were two parts to the anchorage: Great Nore, about half a mile wide and four miles long, was in the main stream, northwest of the town of Sheerness, and Little Nore was a smaller anchorage just off the town.

   The Nore was the site of a mutiny that broke out in May 1797, toward the end of the large-scale mutiny at Spithead. The latter was a relatively restrained and well-organized rebellion that resulted in better pay and working conditions for seamen. In contrast, the mutiny at the Nore, led by Richard Parker of HMS *Sandwich*, collapsed

Exeter Change, Strand, looking westward. " 'The duchy of Lancaster, sir. From Cecil Street to the other side of Exeter Change it is part of the duchy, neither London nor Westminster, and the law is different—writs not the same as London writs: why, even the chapel is a royal peculiar' " (Adam Scriven to Jack Aubrey in *Post Captain*, p. 192).

after a month with no gains, and Parker and twenty-four others were convicted by court-martial and hanged.

Plymouth

An English seaport and naval base in South Devon at the western end of the English Channel. It sits on the estuaries of the Tamar and Plym rivers, which form a natural harbor. Serving as a port since 1311, Plymouth was the starting point for many sea explorations and enterprises, especially during the reign of Elizabeth I. Sir Francis Drake sailed from Plymouth on his voyage around the world in 1577, and it was the base for the fleet that defeated the Spanish Armada in 1588. In 1620 the Pilgrims set out from Plymouth in the *Mayflower* on their voyage to America. Plymouth's naval dockyard was established in 1689.

Ships are guided into Plymouth's harbor by the famed Eddystone Light. The tower that was built in 1755 was designed by John Smeaton, whose dovetailed stone

Plymouth, England. Plymouth, a large, considerable seaport in the west of England, lies at the conflux of the rivers Tamer and Plym, 44 miles west of Exeter, the capital of the county of Devon, and 218 miles west by south of London. This view of Plymouth Dock was taken from Mount Edgecumbe. (Spring 1812 edition of *The Naval Chronicle*, p. 416.)

A chart of Plymouth Sound. This chart of Plymouth Sound, with a delineation of the plan of the dyke or breakwater, forming therein, for shelter to ships at that anchorage, which was laid before the House of Commons, is here presented to the readers of *The Naval Chronicle*, upon a reduced scale. The fidelity with which the reduction has been made, by Mr. Rowe (map and chart engraver of Bedford Street, London) will be found highly creditable to his talents. (Fall 1812 edition of *The Naval Chronicle*, p. 332.)

blocks became the standard for lighthouses that must survive the pounding of waves. It was replaced by the present tower in 1882.

Portsmouth

A seaport and naval base in Hampshire, England, on the island of Portsea in the English Channel. Portsmouth's importance as a naval base derives from its fine harbor, its anchorage protected by the Isle of Wight, and its position across the Channel from France. Britain's first royal dock was built at Portsmouth in 1496 by Henry VII, though the port was in use long before then. In the seventeenth, eighteenth, and nineteenth centuries, as Britain's naval power increased, the dockyard grew and Portsmouth became the most important naval station in the country. The *Victory*, Lord Nelson's flagship at Trafalgar, is preserved in a dry dock at Portsmouth.

Saint-Valéry

A seaport in northern France at the mouth of the Somme River. Saint-Valéry was the point of departure for William the Conqueror when he invaded England in 1066.

Sussex

A county in southern England, between Hampshire and Kent, on the English Channel. An Anglo-Saxon kingdom believed to have been founded in 477, Sussex fell to the kings of Wessex in the ninth century. The Battle of Hastings was fought in Sussex on October 14, 1066.

Toulon

France's chief naval base and dockyard on the Mediterranean coast, thirty miles east of Marseille. Toulon was involved in many skirmishes between the French and the British. In 1793 French Royalists turned this major naval base and arsenal over to an Anglo-Spanish fleet, but Napoleon, then a young artillery colonel, succeeded in driving them out and was rewarded with a promotion to brigadier general. Reestablished as a chief French naval base, Toulon was blockaded for long stretches by the British. In 1803 Nelson was given command of the Toulon blockade, and although he failed to prevent the French from breaking out and uniting with the Spanish fleet, he eventually defeated their combined navies at the Battle of Trafalgar on October 21, 1805.

Wapping Dock

A dock on the north bank of the Thames in the district of Wapping in East London. Extensive blocks of riverside warehouses were built in Wapping in the early nineteenth century, and a series of docks were opened along the Thames to help relieve crowding in the Pool of London, between the Tower and London Bridge. The West India Docks opened in 1802; London Dock and the East India Docks opened in 1805; and the Surrey Commercial Docks opened in 1807.

A Lively Time in the Med
and a Surprise Voyage to
the East Indies

At the opening of book 3, *HMS Surprise*, Aubrey—like his hero Nelson before him—is off blockading Toulon, France's principal Mediterranean naval seaport. Commanding the frigate *Lively*, Aubrey is part of the inshore squadron cruising in the Gulf of Giens, frequently within sight of the shore. Meanwhile, in London, the powers that be are contriving to disenfranchise Aubrey, Maturin, and the captains of the frigates *Indefatigable*, *Medusa*, and *Amphion* of the fortune they took from the Spanish at the end of *Post Captain*.

Before leaving the southeast coast of France to rendezvous with Maturin off Pt. Fornells on the north coast of Minorca, Aubrey orchestrates a raid on Port-Vendres, just north of the east coast of Spain, and discovers the rather unsavory but effective fighting technique of his Chinese and Malay shipmates. He then sails for a nighttime meeting with Maturin, where he discovers that the doctor, for reasons beyond his control, is unable to join the ship. His friend clearly being in need of some assistance in disengaging himself from undesirable company, Aubrey arranges a surprise visit to Port Mahon, now under Spanish control, and a personal escort for the doctor away from Minorca.

NEXT PAGE: En route to Kampong with the king's envoy, the *Surprise* battles a fierce storm south of the Cape of Good Hope. She sails north to Bombay to refit and then continues on to the Far East. On the homeward passage, Maturin discovers a previously unknown giant land tortoise, which he names *Testudo aubreii* in honor of his particular friend.

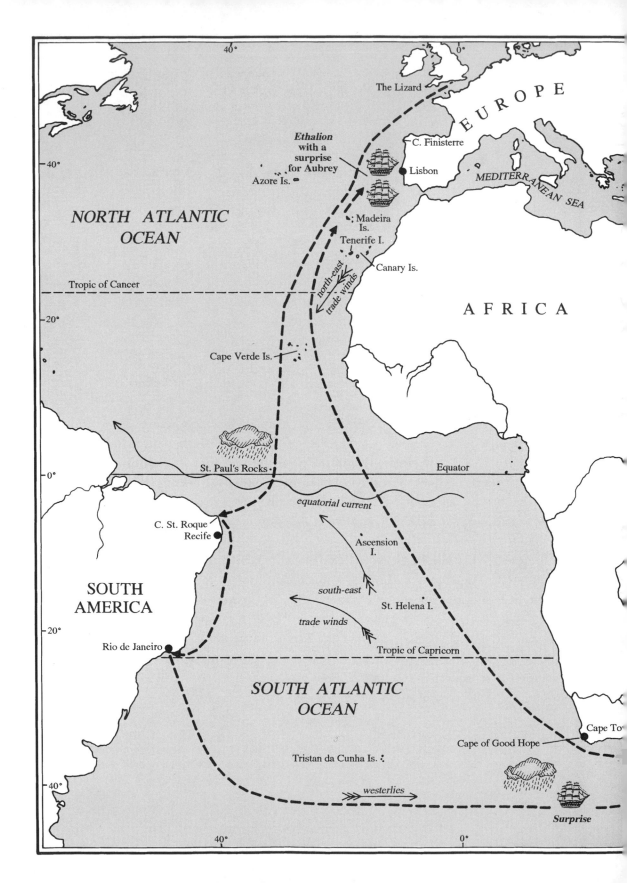

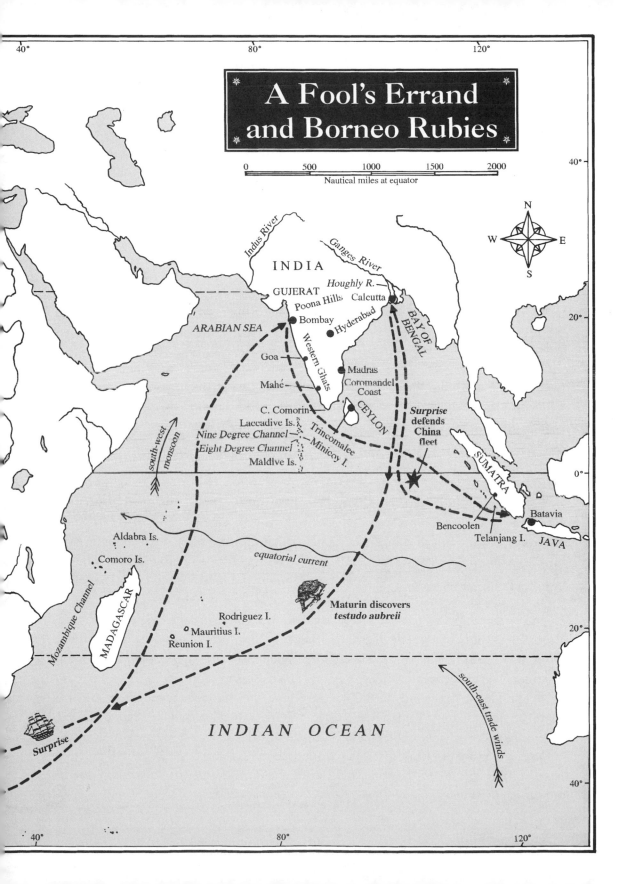

Back in England, Maturin convalesces in Bath while Aubrey spends time in a London debtors' jail. Through the influence of Maturin's intelligence liaison, Sir Joseph Blaine, a commission aboard the *Surprise* is arranged for Aubrey. Since the ship is already saddled with pressing orders to deliver the king's envoy, Stanhope, to Kampong, in the East Indies, talk turns to such exotic subjects as the heat of the Hooghly, the westernmost branch of the Ganges River, which flows through Calcutta and enters the Bay of Bengal.

After facing both malevolent calms and furious storms in the Atlantic, the *Surprise* weathers Cape St. Roque, Brazil, and enters the harbor at Rio de Janeiro, where she is remade in the fleeter image that Aubrey desires. From Rio she heads south to the forties and east, surviving a great storm on the high South Atlantic, rounding the Dutch-controlled Cape of Good Hope, and heading north toward Madagascar. The Surprises ride the southwest monsoon through the Arabian Sea up to India, where they refit at Bombay, on the west coast.

With rumors rife concerning the whereabouts of the French squadron commanded by Linois, the *Surprise* now sails down the coast of India and heads east to the Sunda Strait, which will carry her into the Java Sea. But because Stanhope is ill, she is forced to touch along the south coast of Sumatra. The sheltered anchorage they find, giving access to a jungle-besieged beach, has a bottom that Pullings promises is "as clean as [that near] Gurnard Point," the promontory on the southeast coast of Cornwall, north of Land's End.

And it is in the direction of Cornwall that the *Surprise* is now unexpectedly bound, with a call at Calcutta on the way. But once again, duty intervenes. In latitude 89°E, the *Surprise* meets the British China fleet, heavily laden East Indiamen, many of them capable of making the Canton-to-London voyage nonstop. Two days after joining the merchantmen for a festive meal, the *Surprise* encounters the predatory squadron of Linois, including the frigates *Belle Poule* and *Sémillante*, the 74-gun, two-decker *Marengo*, and the 22-gun corvette *Berceau*, headed on a course that would intercept the China fleet. Aubrey attempts a variety of ruses de guerre to deceive Linois, but the experienced admiral is too cunning to fall for his tricks. Finally, after much maneuvering, the action is decided in a bloody dance between the *Surprise* and Linois's seventy-four.

The China fleet limps into Calcutta, where the Surprises receive a hero's welcome. Homeward bound at last, the *Surprise* weathers the Cape of Good Hope and sails within signaling distance of St. Helena Island, a British colony in the South Atlantic and Napoleon's future place of exile. From a hundred miles off, the Surprises see the grand peak of Tenerife, in the Canary Islands, but they don't stop until they reach Funchal, the capital of Madeira.

A villa on the northeast shore of the harbor of Rio de Janeiro. Opposite the metropolitan city of Saint Sebastian, Chacra-Braganza—the adjunct "Braganza" denoting its being a royal domain—was spontaneously bestowed on Admiral Sir Sidney Smith by the Prince of Brasil [Dom João, the prince regent of Portugal, son of the insane Queen Maria II, who took the title while in exile in Brazil] in commemoration of the 29th of November 1807 [the date that the Portuguese royal family, including Dom João and Queen Maria, among many others, escaped from Cadiz and sailed under Smith's protection to Brazil], and to demonstrate to the world the light in which his royal highness regards services, which in this country appear not to receive any remuneration or acknowledgment beyond a letter from the Secretary of the Admiralty conveying the approbation of the Lords-commissioners. In addition to the picturesque merits of the view, it is presumed that it will be regarded by naval men with a more particular interest as representing a memorial of the gratitude of the reigning house of Braganza towards a distinguished member of their profession. (Fall 1813 edition of *The Naval Chronicle*, p. 48.)

HERE AND THERE

Bombay

A city and port on the Arabian Sea in western India. Until the nineteenth century when the alluvial lowlands were drained to form one island, the city was spread among seven islands just off the mainland: Girgaum (where the East India Company fort was located), Oldman's Island, Colaba, Mazagaon, Parel, Mahim, and Worli. The area first

St. Helena. St. Helena was taken from the Dutch by Sir Richard Munden and then given by King Charles II to the East India Company in 1661, whose property it has remained ever since. In the midst of the vast southern ocean, it is the most distant island from the Continent of any in the known world. The extreme length of St. Helena is not more than nine miles; and its figure is nearly circular, the utmost of its circumference can not be more than 27 miles. It is thought strange by many that so small a spot should not be more frequently missed by ships bound to it, two only having done so in memory; but the caution navigators take in approaching it accounts for their success. As all homeward-bound East India ships touch here, they fall into its parallel of latitude about 50 or 60 leagues to the east of it, lie by all night, for fear of running past, and when day appears, steer due west till they make the land.

The only two landing places are at Rupert's and James's Valleys. In Rupert's Valley, towards the sea, stands a strong fort with heavy cannon, but the valley is not habitable, because it has no water. In the entrance of James's Valley stands James's Fort, the residence of the Governor. This fort defends the valley by a very fine line of 32 pounders and is flanked by a high inaccessible battery on the rocks called "Mundens," under which all ships must pass that come to an anchor before the town. On each side of this valley is a row of handsome sashed houses, forming a regular pretty street; and at the end is a pleasant walk of near a quarter of a mile in length, between a vista of trees, which are always green and blowing.

The number of soldiers on the island is small, never amounting to more than 400 men. This force is far from being sufficient in case of an attack. But every man on the island is trained to arms, and the proper parties are appointed to alarm posts, which they occupy with the greatest alertness whenever the signals are made for that purpose. (Spring 1801 edition of *The Naval Chronicle*, p. 157.)

came under European control in 1534, when it was acquired by the Portuguese. In 1661 it was ceded to the British as part of the dowry of the wife of Charles II, who granted control of Bombay to the British East India Company in 1668. The company established a fort there and made Bombay its Indian headquarters in 1672.

Calcutta

A city and port in eastern India on the Hooghly River, ninety miles north of the Bay of Bengal. Calcutta was founded by the British East India Company, which in 1690 secured from the Mogul emperor Aurangzeb permission to build a settlement on a muddy flatland of the Hooghly. In 1756 Siraj-ud-daula, the nawab of Bengal, captured the British garrison at Calcutta and imprisoned the defenders in a tiny airless room—the infamous Black Hole of Calcutta—where most of them stifled to death. In 1757 the British, under Colonel Robert Clive and Admiral Charles Watson, retook the city. Calcutta served as the capital of British India from 1773 to 1912.

Canary Islands

A group of volcanic islands in the Atlantic Ocean, seventy miles off the northwest coast of Africa. The group is made up of seven large islands—Gran Canaria, Tenerife, Gomera, Hierro, La Palma, Fuerteventura, and Lanzarote—and a few mostly uninhabited smaller islands. "Canary" (from the Latin *canis*) comes from the name originally used for the large wild dogs once found on the islands and later given to the small greenish yellow birds still found there.

Known to the Romans as the "Fortunate Isles," the Canaries were thought to be the western limit of the world. The islands had been forgotten when the Portuguese rediscovered them in 1341. They came under Spanish rule in 1479 and became a popular stop for Spanish vessels trading with the New World. In 1797 the Canaries were the site of one of the few defeats Nelson ever suffered. It was during this battle at Santa Cruz de Tenerife—in a failed attempt to capture a Spanish treasure ship—that he lost his right arm.

Gulf of Giens

An inlet on the Mediterranean coast of France between Cape Sicié, west of Toulon, and the Giens Peninsula, east of the city.

India

The British Empire in India was established by the British East India Company in the seventeenth century. The company conducted its trading activities at "factories," or trading posts, at Madras, Bombay, and Calcutta. The French East India Company, run by the French government and based in Pondicherry, got off to a slower start and never reached a trade volume comparable to that of the British. Nevertheless, rivalry between the two led to war in the eighteenth century. The British emerged victorious, and the British East India Company began to make extensive territorial acquisitions. But allegations of corruption and misrule led Parliament to pass the Regulating Act of 1773 and the India Act of 1784, which gave the government greater control of India. In the nineteenth century, the company began to see a gradual reduction of its privileges. Its trade monopoly was abolished in 1813, and by 1858 India was under the direct rule of the British Crown.

Madeira
The largest of the Madeira Islands, a volcanic archipelago in the Atlantic Ocean four hundred miles west of Morocco. The archipelago is comprised of Madeira and Porto Santo as well as two groups of small, uninhabited islands called Desertas and Selvagens. Explored by the Phoenicians and the Genoese, Madeira was colonized in 1420 by Portuguese navigator João Goncalves Zarco, who founded Funchal, the capital, in 1421. The British occupied Madeira for a short time in 1801 and again from 1807 to 1814. The island is famous for its several varieties of fortified wines, one of which was sometimes used medicinally.

Norman Cross
A prisoner-of-war camp in Cambridgeshire, where some eighteen hundred French soldiers and sailors died in captivity. During the Napoleonic wars a popular—and profitable—pastime for French prisoners was carving model ships from the bones of the mutton they were fed. A great number of these exquisite models were made at Norman Cross.

St. Paul's Rocks
A group of volcanic rocks in the Atlantic Ocean, about six hundred miles northeast of Cape St. Roque, Brazil.

Tenerife
The largest of the Canary Islands, about forty miles northwest of Grand Canary. Its capital, Santa Cruz de Tenerife, was founded in 1494. The mountainous island has a precipitous coast and rises to 12,200 feet at Pico de Teide.

Action in the Indian Ocean

When *The Mauritius Command* opens, Aubrey, back in the South Downs at Ashgrove Cottage, is suffering domestic life—especially his obnoxious mother-in-law—poorly. Broke and without a commission, he ponders the stars and planets and, wistfully, the Portsmouth harbor, which is visible over the hill separating Ashgrove from the coast. But Aubrey's luck is about to change for the better. The Spanish have recently entered the war against France, and Maturin—who rides over to Ashgrove from his lodgings at the Crown in Petersfield, on the main Portsmouth-to-London road—has brought his influence to bear in favor of his particular friend.

Commissioned on board the *Boadicea*, Aubrey sails for the Indian Ocean accompanied by William Farquhar, whom he is to ensconce as governor of Mauritius—that is, once Aubrey takes Mauritius from the French. On the way he takes the French *Hébé*, formerly the British *Hyaena*, and her prize, the British snow *Intrepid Fox*. This fortunate action not only promises to provide Aubrey with some much-needed income, but it also allows him to improve the crew of *Boadicea* by pressing some Foxes and by repatriating the *Hébé*'s British prisoners. At the same time, Aubrey sends lowly members of his own ship, including part of the draft from Bedfordshire, a landlocked county north of Lon-

NEXT PAGE: Aubrey is made commodore of a squadron that is to restore the balance of power in the Indian Ocean. Shuttling between the Cape and the islands, he employs a hodgepodge of ships and British troops from India to battle the French.

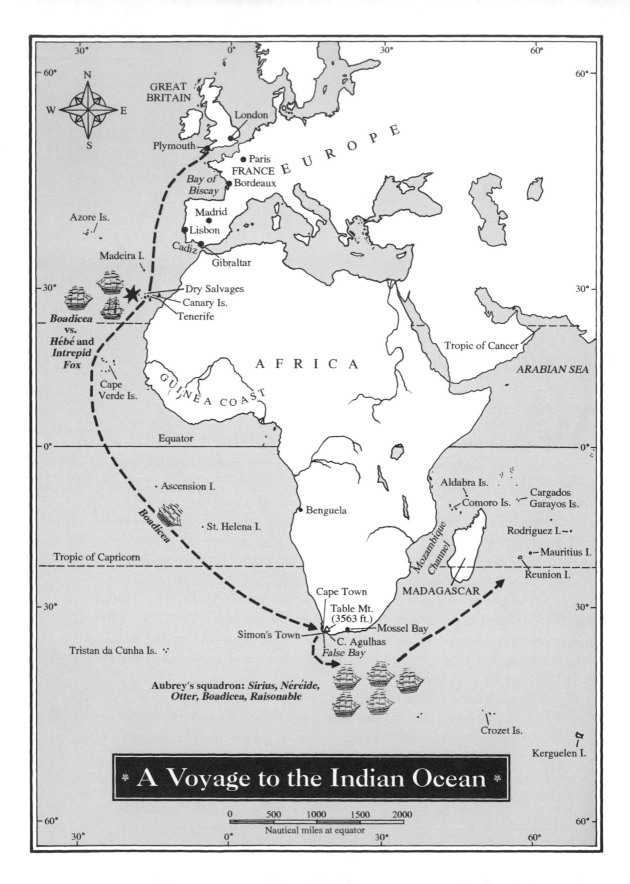

❋ A Voyage to the Indian Ocean ❋

don, off to Gibraltar in the prize. During the rest of the trip to the Cape of Good Hope, Aubrey works his crew into an efficient fighting machine.

In Simon's Bay, an inlet in the larger False Bay on the east coast of the Cape peninsula, Admiral Bertie officially makes Aubrey commodore of a squadron that will base at the tiny island of Rodriguez, about 350 miles east of Mauritius in the Indian Ocean. His squadron consists of the frigates *Sirius*, commanded by Captain Pym, and *Néréide*, under Captain Corbett, and the sloop *Otter*, commanded by Lord Clonfert, a former shipmate of Aubrey's. Aubrey hoists his flag in the *Raisonable*, a large, old ship of the line, while Captain Eliot takes command of the *Boadicea*.

The squadron sails north to La Réunion, where Maturin makes a nighttime reconnaissance mission and learns the location of some recently captured Indiamen as well as the strength of the French troops and fortifications. Aubrey sails northeast to the island of Rodriguez and persuades British Lieutenant-Colonel Keating that his troops should join Aubrey's squadron in an invasion of La Réunion. St. Paul on the northwest coast is the initial target. Landing Keating's troops at a point seven miles north of the town, Aubrey sets his battle plan in motion.

Following the action at St. Paul's, Aubrey leaves part of his squadron to blockade Mauritius and returns to the Cape, where he ditches the weak-kneed *Raisonable* and shifts his pendant to the newly cleaned and refitted *Boadicea*. Despite Aubrey's success at La Réunion, the military bureaucracy at the Cape prevents him from returning to deliver a swift and definitive blow to the French, who, with several strong frigates on the prowl, still have the upper hand in the Indian Ocean. With a new squadron, Aubrey at last sails for Mauritius, gaining the frigate *Magicienne*, commanded by Lucius Curtis, en route.

While Maturin, aided by Lord Clonfert, who now commands the *Néréide*, covertly undermines the French on La Réunion, the rest of the squadron blockades Port St. Louis, on the northwest coast of Mauritius. After a fierce storm brings an end to that enterprise, the squadron returns to the Cape once again to refit. This time, in Simon's Bay, Aubrey's squadron gains Captain Lambert's 36-gun frigate *Iphigenia*—which brings the welcome news that British military reinforcements from Madras have landed at La Réunion—and the unloved, aged 50-gun *Leopard*.

The wheels are now set in motion for the invasion of La Réunion. Thomas Pullings, captain of the transport brig *Groper*, joins the squadron at Rodriguez, where the battle strategy is laid with Colonel Keating. The plan calls for landings on either side of the town of St. Denis, the island's capital, lying on the north coast. In a rough surf, Aubrey's squadron lands the troops, losing many of the landing boats and several men on a rocky, surf-pounded shore. Maturin, the diplomat, also pursues his own plan of action.

The consensus among the commodore, the redcoat commanders, and the new governor, Farquhar, is that the next blow, that to Mauritius, must be delivered posthaste, not just while French morale is low but before any uninformed British orders can arrive from afar. As Aubrey explains to Maturin, the plan is to surprise the French by taking Port South-East, on the southeastern coast of Mauritius, not the capital, Port St. Louis, in the northwest, which they have been blockading. To take Port South-East, the squadron must first secure the heavily fortified Ile de la Passe at the mouth of the port's tortuous and shallow harbor.

Once this is done and the returning French squadron—including the *Victor,* the *Minerve,* the *Bellone,* and the prize *Ceylon,* an Indiaman—battles its way into Port South-East, the stage is nearly set for a showdown at Mauritius. Here, among the treacherous shoals of Port South-East, the *Néréide, Sirius,* and *Magicienne* fight to the bitter end.

With his squadron now reduced, Aubrey—greatly outnumbered but undaunted—plays cat and mouse with Commodore Hamelin's French, trading and retrading ships in the waters surrounding Mauritius and La Réunion. But Aubrey gradually restores the balance of power and pieces together an attack force. With a refitted squadron and his final goal in sight, the commodore is bearing down on Mauritius when suddenly a new force is introduced into the theater—nothing less than a "bleeding armada," as the *Boadicea*'s lookout puts it. For all practical purposes, the fight for Mauritius is over.

HERE AND THERE

Ashgrove Cottage

The house in Hampshire where Jack Aubrey resides with his wife Sophie, their children Charlotte, Fanny, and George, and often with his irascible mother-in-law Mrs. Williams. While the large, comfortable homes of more fortunate sea officers might overlook Portsmouth and the Channel, Ashgrove "stood low on a cold, damp slope facing north, on poor, spewy soil, with no means of access but a hollow lane, deep in mud much of the year and impassable after heavy rain."

Still, on a good day the grounds of Ashgrove, with its plentiful ash trees, can be considered picturesque, even romantic, and Aubrey manages to erect an observatory that allows him to peer down at the shipping in and about Portsmouth and the Isle of Wight. Likewise, he makes the best of his low-ceilinged home and isolated grounds by adding on additions and building impressive stables for his prize mounts. And despite

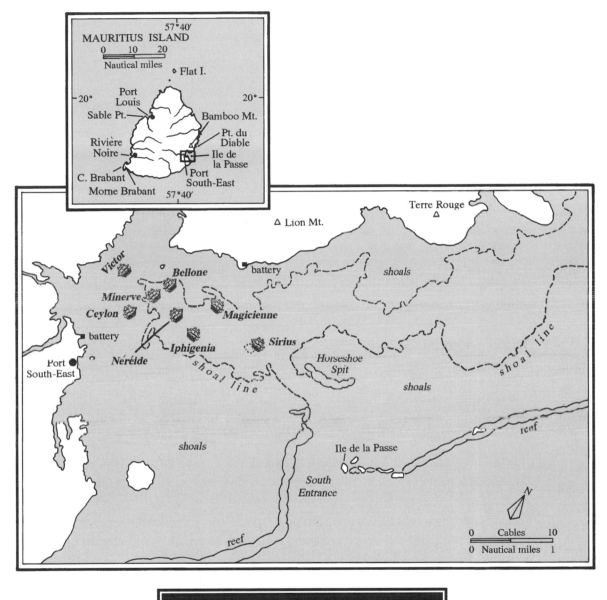

Warm Work in Shallow Waters

MAURITIUS ISLAND
57°40'
0 10 20
Nautical miles
Flat I.
20°
Port Louis
Sable Pt.
Bamboo Mt.
Pt. du Diable
Rivière Noire
Ile de la Passe
C. Brabant
Port South-East
Morne Brabant
57°40'
20°

Terre Rouge
Lion Mt.
Victor
Bellone
battery
shoals
Minerve
Ceylon
Magicienne
battery
Sirius
Iphigenia
Néréide
Port South-East
shoal line
Horseshoe Spit
shoals
shoal line
shoals
Ile de la Passe
reef
South Entrance
N
reef
0 Cables 10
0 Nautical miles 1

The French score a victory in Port South-East, Mauritius. Near the close of the action, depicted here, the British ships *Sirius*, *Magicienne*, and *Iphigenia* have run aground. Along with the shore batteries, the French ships *Ceylon*, *Minerve*, and *Bellone* pummel the vulnerable *Néréide*.

its remote setting, Ashgrove has convenient access to the main Portsmouth-to-London road at the nearby towns of Petersfield, Buriton, and Cosham.

Cape of Good Hope

A rocky peninsula jutting into the Atlantic Ocean near the southern tip of Africa. Rising in a sheer cliff 840 feet above the ocean, the cape was thought by early sailors to be the extreme southern point of the continent, which actually lies ninety miles to the southwest at Cape Agulhas. The Cape, with its hazardous winds and currents, was originally named the Cape of Storms by Portuguese navigator Bartolomeu Dias, who first sighted it in 1488. It was given its present name—either by Dias or by King John II of Portugal—in reaction to the riches of Oriental trade that flowed around it. The Dutch settled nearby Table Bay in 1652, and the British took control of the area in 1795. It reverted to the Dutch in 1803, but the British retook it in 1806.

Dry Salvages

Also known as the Selvagens, a group of barren, uninhabited islets in the Canary Islands.

Eight Degree Channel

A passage in the Indian Ocean between the Maldive Islands and Minicoy Island. The channel is named for its location at 8°N latitude.

Mauritius

A volcanic island surrounded by coral reefs, five hundred miles east of Madagascar in the Indian Ocean. With La Réunion and Rodriguez, it makes up the Mascarene Islands. Mauritius was discovered by the Portuguese in 1510 and colonized by the Dutch in the seventeenth century. In 1721 the French, who called the island Ile de France, established a settlement there, setting up sugar plantations and bringing in East African slaves to work on them. French privateers also used Mauritius as a base from which they attacked British East Indiamen in the Indian Ocean. After an unsuccessful blockade, the British captured the island in 1810.

"Fatal experience has proved, that no position could be more successfully adapted to the annoyance of British commerce in the Indian seas than the Mauritius while in the possession of France," it is noted in the spring edition of *The Naval Chronicle* for 1811. "It served as a place of rendezvous for French frigates, where they could be refitted, and whither they might retire with their plunder. It was a *depôt* of captured produce, in which view it was resorted to by American traders, who brought that produce to Europe which the French were unable to convey in their own merchantmen. The destruction

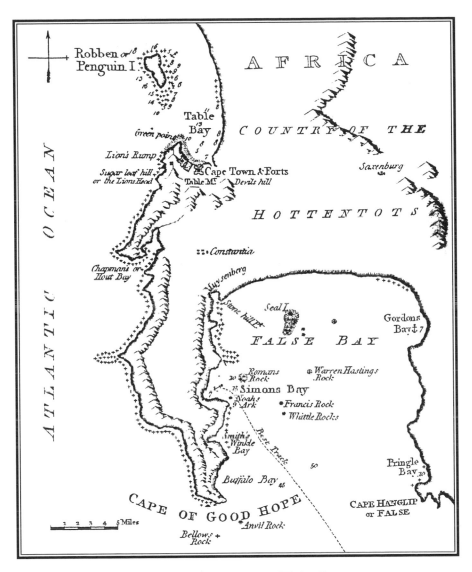

A chart of Cape of Good Hope, Table Bay, and False Bay.

of such a nest of marauders is an immense advantage to be derived from the conquest of the island which, in our hands, is impregnable, as long as we command the seas, and may, perhaps, be rendered a station of some importance" (p. 144).

Mauritius and the other Mascarene Islands are also known for being the home of the dodo bird, a stout, flightless bird resembling the turkey but related to the pigeon.

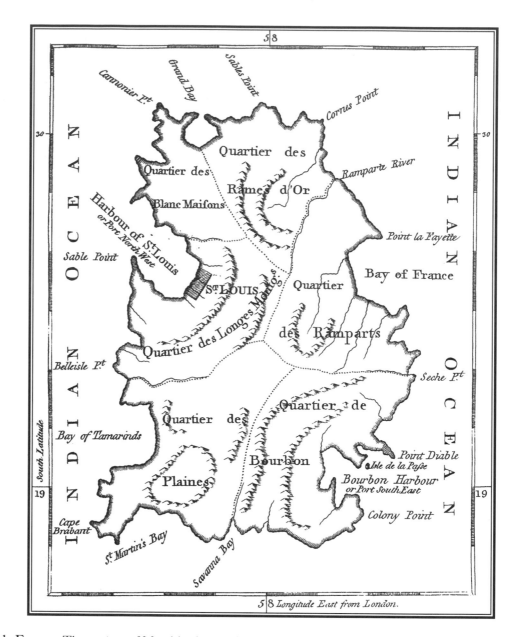

A chart of Isle de France. The capture of Mauritius is one of those achievements that demonstrates what can be done by the united efforts of the Navy and Army. It demonstrates the sort of enterprise, which—given our insular situation and our maritime superiority—we are sure ultimately to succeed in and to which our resources ought to be applied. All foreign expeditions not undertaken by floating armies, or in other words, by the combination of naval and military operations, can be considered inconsistent with our real character. This is the type of assistance, which one of the three noble lords considered to be the head of parliamentary opposition, alluded, in speaking of the service to be rendered to allies, instead of making ourselves principals in the internal warfare of the Peninsula. In the House of Commons, on the 13th of February, the member for Bedford is reported to have said: "The Isle of France is certainly an important conquest—the most important of all our colonial conquests since the commencement of the war." (Spring 1811 edition of *The Naval Chronicle*, p. 144.)

Each island had its own species, but they were all extinct by 1800. They were easy prey for hunters and lost their eggs to the pigs, rats, and dogs introduced by the settlers.

Ten Degree Channel

A passage between the Andaman Islands and the Nicobar Islands, in the eastern Bay of Bengal, so named for its position at 10°N latitude.

From Hot Water in Hampshire to Shattering South Seas

Desolation Island opens at Ashgrove Cottage, the Aubrey home in Hampshire, amid a flurry of activity and, for Jack, mounting domestic pressures, including a dangerous new business relationship with the charlatan Kimber. By chapter three, however, Aubrey and Maturin, who has suffered his own share of land-borne woes, are once again safely at sea, this time on board the *Leopard,* a 50-gun fourth-rate, heading around the globe to New South Wales, a British colony in what is today Australia.

Aubrey's mission involves the nonfictional William Bligh, the ill-fated captain of the *Bounty,* who in 1808, as governor of New South Wales, suffered another mutiny and was imprisoned. Aubrey has been sent to restore order. Just before setting sail, the Admiralty also saddled the two-decker *Leopard* with a shipment of prisoners, including the young American spy Louisa Wogan, for delivery to a penal colony in New South Wales. Afterward, as Aubrey tells Maturin, the *Leopard* will join Admiral Drury in the neighborhood of Penang, an island near Sumatra.

With the coast of Spain lurking nearby to leeward, the *Leopard* battles a northwesterly gale in the Bay of Biscay, a body of water infamous among sailors for its ferocious storms. The seas grow so violent that two of the convicts die from seasickness. After weathering the storm, the *Leopard* picks up the northeast trade winds early and sails swiftly across the Tropic of Cancer, passing Madeira and the Canary Islands before resupplying at Porto Praya, St. Jago (São Tiago), the largest of the Cape Verde Islands, which lie about three hundred miles off the west coast of Africa.

A view of Fort Cornwallis on Prince of Wales's Island, or Penang. This island off the west coast of the Malay peninsula was ceded by the King of Queda to the East India Company, and from its natural advantages and from the circumstance of a British colony having been formed there, it has of late acquired considerable importance. In 1786 the first British settlement of the Malay peninsula was formed at Georgetown on this island. (Spring 1813 edition of *The Naval Chronicle*, p. 52.)

The Leopards' good luck is short-lived, however, for the trades not only begin early, but die early. The ship drifts for several weeks in the doldrums just above the equator. During this frustrating time, a strange gaol-fever devastates the crew. Maturin convinces Aubrey to touch at Brazil to drop off two dozen of the dying and to acquire greenstuff and more medicine before pressing on to Simon's Town, the British settlement just south of Cape Town at the tip of what is today South Africa.

In Recife, Brazil, South America's easternmost port and a popular stopping point for ships bound for the South Atlantic, Aubrey learns that the *Waakzaamheid*, a Dutch seventy-four, recently engaged a British frigate, the *Nymph*, in nearby waters. Aubrey becomes convinced that the *Waakzaamheid* is bound in the same direction as the *Leopard* in order to defend Holland's colonies in the East Indies. This intimidating foe does, in fact, appear one morning on the horizon. The dogged pursuit that follows drives the *Leopard* southward into the tempestuous seas of the lower forties. Like a ghost ship, *Waakzaamheid* disappears and resurfaces, always between the *Leopard* and her destination, the southern tip of Africa. Finally, in a driving storm, the two ships battle sternchaser to bow-chaser in the troughs and peaks of a dark, pitching sea.

At the conclusion of this action, the *Leopard* finds herself in lonely waters too far south and east to pursue her original course to the Cape. Aubrey decides to take advantage of the prevailing westerlies and sail directly for Botany Bay, about five thousand miles away. But the *Leopard* has only a ton of water left, the rest having been started in

Porto Praya, St. Jago, Cape Verde. Porto Praya has long been a place where the outward-bound Guinea and Indiamen (whether English, French, or Dutch) have touched for water and refreshments. The gaol is the best building and next to that the church. The Governor resides in a small wooden barrack at the extremity of the plain, commanding a view of the bay and shipping. Earl Macartney, on his embassy, was received by him with due honor and respect, but as he had shared in the general wretchedness caused by the long drought, he had neither wine nor any other refreshments to offer. (Spring 1811 edition of *The Naval Chronicle*, p. 233.)

the chase, so he heads farther south to gather ice for drinking. Maturin, searching excitedly for sea leopards and other regional fauna, revels in his first trip to antarctic waters. But a heavy fog and treacherous ice-laden sea cut his pleasure short. The *Leopard* is driven upon the ice. This fictional event is based on Lieutenant Edward Riou's historic voyage from the Cape of Good Hope to Australia in December of 1789. En route, after collecting ice for drinking purposes near the then unknown Prince Edward Islands, his ship, the *Guardian*, struck an iceberg. Riou allowed the officers and men who wanted to leave the ship to do so in boats, but he and sixty-one devotees remained on board to attempt to salvage the *Guardian*, which they eventually did.

As Aubrey's *Leopard* founders, First Lieutenant Grant and other skeptics, hoping to travel nearly fifteen hundred miles northwest to the Cape, depart in two of the ship's cutters. Those who remain, driven by an abiding faith in their captain, pump ship around the clock. Lacking a rudder, the heavy ship lumbers eastward, searching for land in a stretch of ocean that is vast and empty. She has two chances: to find either the Crozets, a cluster of five small islands discovered in 1772 by the French explorer Marc Marion-Du Fresne, or the little-known Kerguelen Island, also somewhat ominously called Desolation Island, discovered the same year but thought by Aubrey to be laid down incorrectly. The alternative, as Aubrey puts it, is "to travel on and on, with nothing between her pierced bottom and the antarctic sea but a piece of worn sailcloth."

Although the *Leopard* eventually seeks refuge on what appears to be Kerguelen Island, O'Brian confuses the issue eight books later. In *The Thirteen Gun Salute*, as they pass near Kerguelen Island, Aubrey tells Midshipman Richardson that Kerguelen "is not *our* Desolation Island, which is smaller, farther south and east." That would make it either Heard Island or one of the McDonald Islands, which lie some three hundred miles to the southeast of Kerguelen and were undiscovered until 1853, or fictional.

HERE AND THERE

Cape Finisterre

The westernmost point of Spain, Cape Finisterre is a finger of land jutting into the Atlantic Ocean. Although both names translate as "Land's End," the cape should not be confused with the Finistère department at the extreme northwest tip of France.

Cape Verde Islands

A group of Atlantic islands about three hundred miles west of their namesake, Cape Verde, on the western tip of Africa. The group consists of ten main islands and a number of small, uninhabited islands. Volcanic in origin, they are mostly mountainous with forbidding coasts. The highest point, Cano Peak, rises more than nine thousand feet on the island of Fogo. The Cape Verdes have suffered from severe cyclical droughts since 1747, and many Cape Verdians migrated to the United States after serving on New England whaling ships. In fact, most overseas Cape Verdians still live in coastal towns in Massachusetts.

NEXT PAGE: Pursued by the *Waakzaamheid*, the eastbound *Leopard* is forced farther and farther south into the mountainous swells of the stormy lower forties.

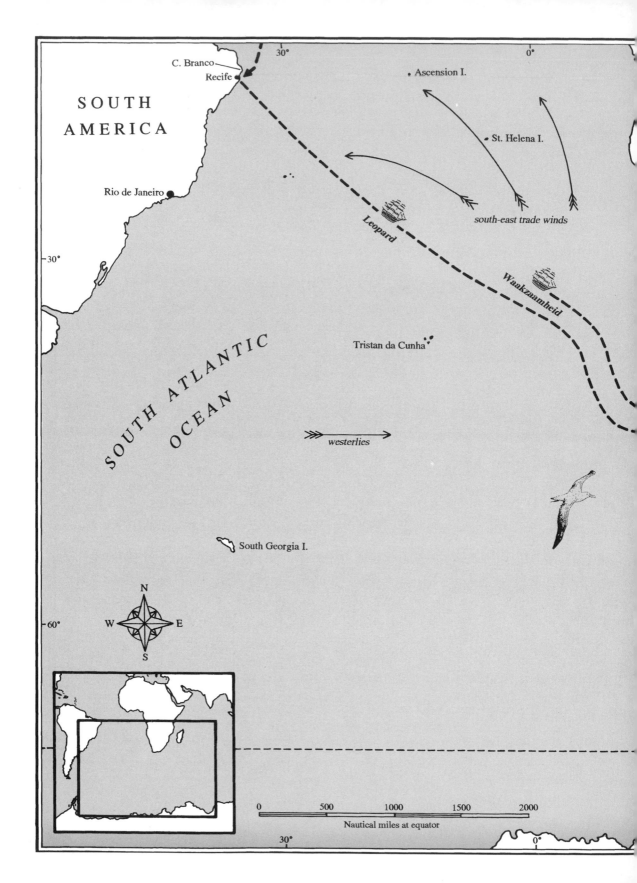

C. Branco
Recife

SOUTH
AMERICA

Rio de Janeiro

30°

30°

Ascension I.

St. Helena I.

south-east trade winds

Leopard

Waakzaamheid

Tristan da Cunha

SOUTH ATLANTIC
OCEAN

westerlies

South Georgia I.

N
W   E
S

60°

0   500   1000   1500   2000
Nautical miles at equator

30°   0°

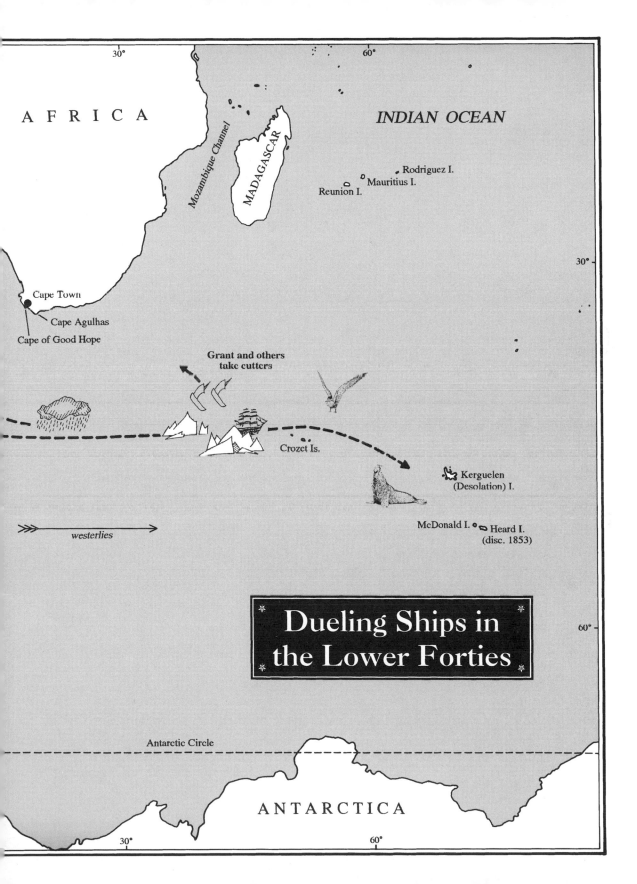

AFRICA

INDIAN OCEAN

Mozambique Channel

MADAGASCAR

• Rodriguez I.
Mauritius I.
Reunion I.

Cape Town
Cape Agulhas
Cape of Good Hope

30°

Grant and others
take cutters

Crozet Is.

Kerguelen
(Desolation) I.

McDonald I. Heard I.
(disc. 1853)

westerlies

60°

**Dueling Ships in
the Lower Forties**

Antarctic Circle

ANTARCTICA

30°

60°

A view of the Peak of Fogo, or del Fuego. The Peak of Fogo, or del Fuego, the highest of the Cape Verde Islands, is said to be a constantly burning volcano. Voyagers have asserted that it is visible at above 100 miles. The atmosphere was hazy when the accompanying sketch was taken, which was perhaps the reason the eruption was not seen. (Fall 1814 edition of *The Naval Chronicle*, p. 58.)

The islands are believed to have been discovered in 1456 by Alvise Ca'da Mosto, a Venetian explorer commissioned by the Portuguese prince Henry the Navigator. Portuguese settlers arrived in 1462, establishing plantations worked by slaves and creating a commercial center for ships traveling between Africa and South America, especially those involved in the slave trade.

Kerguelen Island

A mountainous island in the south Indian Ocean with a rugged coastline and deep fjords. The island was named after the French navigator Yves-Joseph de Kerguélen-Trémarec, who discovered it in 1772. Captain Cook spent Christmas here in 1776, renaming it the "Island of Desolation." Cook's men must have agreed with his appellation; they described the island as a "cold blustering wet country [with] the melancholy croaking of innumerable penguins."

Recife

An Atlantic seaport in Brazil at the easternmost edge of South America. Recife was first settled in 1535 by the Portuguese, who established sugarcane plantations along the coast and brought in African slaves to work them. The city was sacked by English privateers in 1595 and occupied by the Dutch between 1630 and 1654. Recife has long been an important port of call, especially for ships bound for Cape Horn or the Cape of Good Hope.

An Unlucky Voyage from the East Indies

Looking more like a shabby merchant ship than a man-of-war, HMS *Leopard* sails into the bay of the fictional Pulo Batang near Penang, or Prince of Wales Island, which lies off the west coast of the Malay Peninsula. Aubrey meets with the port admiral, Drury, and recounts the *Leopard's* triumphs and woes in southern waters—the decimation of the crew by gaol-fever, the sinking of the 74-gun Dutch ship *Waakzaamheid*, the near destruction of the *Leopard* by ice, and its eventual repair at Desolation Island.

With the beleaguered *Leopard* now condemned to transport duty and most of her crew to be usurped by the port admiral, Aubrey, Maturin, and some of Aubrey's hand-picked Leopards receive orders to sail for home on board the ship *La Flèche*. In Simon's Bay at the Cape of Good Hope, they discover that America has declared war on England, thereby launching what becomes the War of 1812. But before Aubrey and his shipmates ever have the chance to encounter one of America's powerful frigates, they must survive a perilous adventure on an 18-foot cutter. Nearing Brazil after many days of fine sailing, *La Flèche* settles into a dead calm under a blazing sun. One night she suddenly bursts into flames. The Leopards pile on board a cutter and watch as *La Flèche* burns to the sea. Scorched by the sun and salted by the breeze, they drift for many brutal days before HMS *Java*, a 38-gun frigate, rescues them.

On board the *Java*, Aubrey feasts voraciously, but he also learns of the recent American victories over the Royal Navy. He need not stew in his blue thoughts for long, however. The American heavy frigate *Constitution* is also cruising in Brazilian waters.

Within sight of the coast of Brazil, the *Java* meets the *Constitution*, as it did historically and with the same grim result. (For a diagram of the battle maneuvers, see the inset on the map "Fire, Sun, Lead, and Lunatics," next page.) For the second time on this ill-fated homeward voyage, Aubrey and his shipmates watch their ship perish in flames.

Aubrey draws some small solace from the fact that at least the much-battered *Constitution* has been prevented from cruising to the Pacific, where she had been headed with the goal of becoming a nuisance to British interests in that vast arena. She must return to her home port, Boston, for repairs, and Aubrey holds out hope that she will meet up with one of the blockading British ships off the Chesapeake, near Sandy Hook, New Jersey, or near Boston, where they tended to concentrate. However, this wish goes unrealized.

The British prisoners are taken to Boston, where all chances of a quick parole via Halifax, Nova Scotia, fade for Aubrey. Recovering from a violent case of pneumonia, he convalesces at the Asclepia, a madhouse near Beacon Hill. From his window Aubrey observes through his telescope the American frigates in Boston Harbor and the British

The High Land of Never-sink and Sandy Hook Light House. Sandy Hook is a long point of sand belonging to New Jersey in North America and running northward with considerable curvature westerly so as to form the larboard or southern shore of the entrance to New York. This is a cruising ground for the national pilots and also a customary station of warlike cruisers, of which too, a line of battle ship and a frigate are represented in the place, as employed in the service of blockade. (Spring 1814 edition of *The Naval Chronicle,* p. 320.)

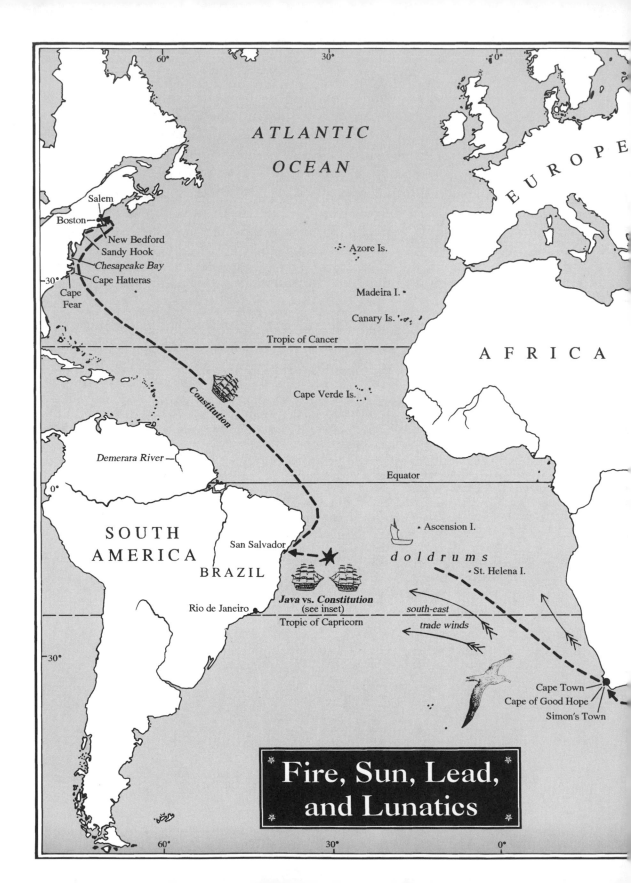

ATLANTIC
OCEAN

Salem
Boston

New Bedford
Sandy Hook
Chesapeake Bay
Cape Hatteras
Cape
Fear

30°

· Azore Is.

Madeira I. ·

Canary Is.

Tropic of Cancer

Constitution

Cape Verde Is.

EUROPE

AFRICA

Demerara River —

0°

SOUTH
AMERICA

BRAZIL

San Salvador

Equator

· Ascension I.

doldrums

· St. Helena I.

Java vs. **Constitution**
(see inset)

Rio de Janeiro

Tropic of Capricorn

south-east

trade winds

30°

Cape Town
Cape of Good Hope
Simon's Town

Fire, Sun, Lead, and Lunatics

60°

30°

0°

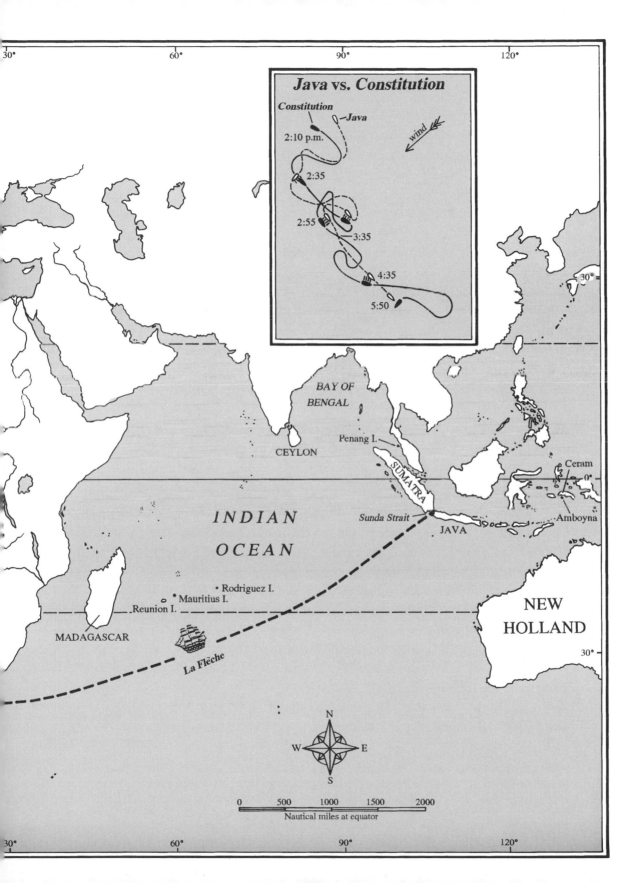

Java vs. Constitution

Constitution —Java

2:10 p.m.

2:35

2:55

3:35

4:35

5:50

wind

BAY OF
BENGAL

Penang I.

CEYLON

SUMATRA

Ceram

Amboyna

INDIAN

OCEAN

Sunda Strait

JAVA

• Rodriguez I.

Mauritius I.

Reunion I.

NEW
HOLLAND

MADAGASCAR

La Flèche

N

W   E

S

0   500   1000   1500   2000
Nautical miles at equator

blockade. His low spirits are further dampened by news of new American victories, like the sinking of the *Peacock* by the *Hornet* off the Demerara River, which flows into the Atlantic in what is today Guyana on the northeast coast of South America.

Maturin, meanwhile, meets a fellow traveler from the *Leopard*, Louisa Wogan, who informs him that Diana Villiers will soon be arriving in Boston with her "particular friend" Harry Johnson, a wealthy Maryland landowner with political ties. Maturin eventually determines that his maneuverings in the name of British intelligence have led to the suspicion that Aubrey is a spy. As the plots unfolds, Maturin engages in a treacherous war of wits with American and French agents in order to extricate himself, Aubrey, and Villiers from this web of intrigue. After a violent end, the three are forced to escape the city in a small boat.

The Fortune of War concludes with a fierce historic naval battle. In an effort to restore the recently tarnished British Naval pride, Captain Philip Broke of HMS *Shannon* issues a challenge via letter to Captain Lawrence of the *Chesapeake*, which is in Boston Harbor. With Aubrey and Maturin on board the *Shannon* and yachts and pleasure boats present to spectate, they meet, like two bare-knuckle prizefighters, in Massachusetts Bay.

HERE AND THERE

Cape Town
A seaport in southwest Africa on Table Bay at the northern end of the Cape Peninsula. Cape Town was founded in 1652 by Jan van Riebeeck to serve as a supply station for the Dutch East India Company ships rounding the Cape of Good Hope. In 1781, amid the turmoil created by the American War of Independence, a British fleet attempted to occupy the Cape, which directors of the English East India Company described as "the Gibralter of India." A French fleet aided the Dutch in repulsing the British. In 1795 it was captured by a British force, but it was returned to the Dutch by the Treaty of Amiens in 1803. In 1806 it again came under British control.

Dutch East Indies
An archipelago of more than three thousand islands in Southeast Asia astride the equator, formerly controlled by the Netherlands and now forming Indonesia. The major

PREVIOUS PAGE: Aubrey, Maturin, and some of their shipmates hitch a ride on board the homeward-bound *La Flèche*, but a series of mishaps prevents a direct passage. Scorched by fire and sun, pierced by lead, and housed with lunatics, they find themselves stuck in Boston.

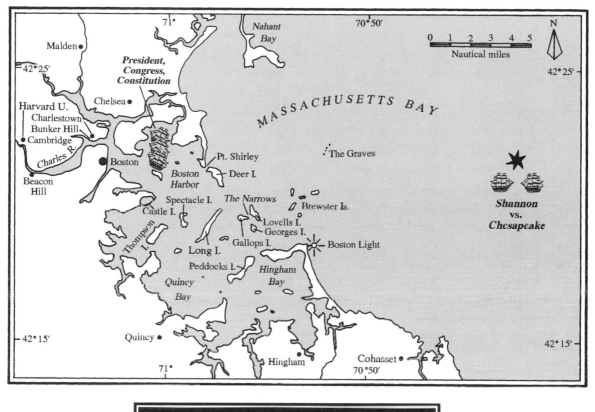

Map labels: Malden • / 42°25' / Harvard U. / Charlestown / Bunker Hill / Cambridge / Beacon Hill / Charles R. / Chelsea • / *President, Congress, Constitution* / Boston / *Boston Harbor* / Spectacle I. / Castle I. / *The Narrows* / Thompson I. / Long I. / Peddocks I. / *Quincy Bay* / Quincy • / 71° / Pt. Shirley / Deer I. / Lovells I. / Georges I. / Gallops I. / *Hingham Bay* / Hingham / Nahant Bay / MASSACHUSETTS BAY / The Graves / Brewster Is. / Boston Light / Cohasset • / 70°50' / 70°50' / N / 0 1 2 3 4 5 Nautical miles / 42°25' / *Shannon* vs. *Chesapeake* / 42°15' / 42°15' / 71°

❋ A Challenge of Honor Accepted ❋

Recognizing a chance to redeem the Royal Navy's bruised reputation, the *Shannon*, with Aubrey and Maturin on board, takes on the *Chesapeake* twenty miles from Boston in a battle based on the historic encounter of June 1, 1813.

islands included Bali, Bangka, part of Borneo, Celebes, Ceram, Flores, Java, Lombok, Madura, and Sumatra. High mountains, some of them volcanic, extend the length of the archipelago.

The islands, which command vital sea routes between Australia, Europe, and the Asian mainland, were controlled by the Dutch East India Company from 1602 until 1798, when they were turned over to the government of the Netherlands (then known as the Batavian Republic), which at the time was a virtual satellite of France. During the Napoleonic wars, much of the territory was seized by the British. The islands were restored to the Netherlands in 1816.

Spice Islands

A group of islands in the Malay Archipelago, between Celebes and New Guinea, now called the Moluccas and forming a province of Indonesia. Cloves from the northern Moluccas and nutmeg from the central islands were traded in Asia long before Europeans heard of the Spice Islands. The Portuguese arrived in 1511, beginning many decades of conflict, first with the reigning sultans and later among the Spanish, English, and Dutch, with the latter eventually triumphing. The struggles for control of the region caused substantial loss of life during this period. The victorious Dutch earned large profits, but by the end of the eighteenth century, the spice trade had greatly diminished, and the Moluccas became an economic backwater.

"Spice Islands" was also sometimes used to refer generally to the Dutch East Indies.

A chart of the Strait of Sunda. Drawn by W. McKellar, master of *HMS Belliqueux*, in 1811, this chart shows, among other identifiable locations: Sumatra, Java Head, Pepper Bay, Prince's Island, Cracatoa Island, Button Island, and Thwart the Way Island. The chart originally appeared in Krusenstern's *Memoir on a Chart of the Strait of Sunda & c* (1813). (Spring 1815 edition of *The Naval Chronicle*, p. 57.)

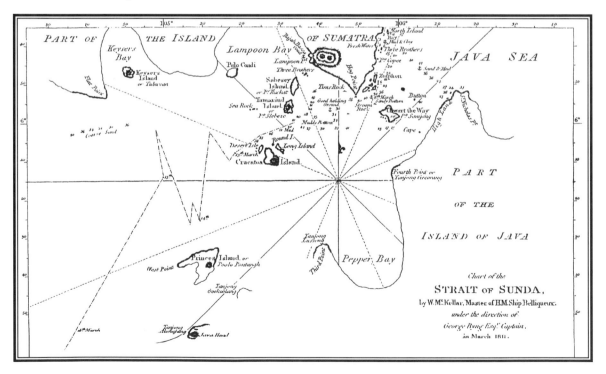

From North America to the Baltic to the Tower in the Temple

O n board the *Shannon* as it sails with its prize, USS *Chesapeake*, Aubrey, Maturin, and Diana Villiers enter the harbor at Halifax, Nova Scotia, a British settlement from 1749 and its key North American military and naval outpost. While the seamen celebrate their much-needed victory, Maturin hands over the documents he obtained in Boston, capping off his own coup in the realm of intelligence.

After attending a lavish ball to celebrate Captain Philip Broke's victory, Aubrey, Maturin, and Villiers depart for England on board the packet *Diligence,* which is preceded by the *Nova Scotia,* a sloop carrying news of the *Shannon*'s victory. Just north of Sable Island, off Nova Scotia, the swift-sailing *Diligence* is spotted by two equally fast American privateers, the *Liberty* and another schooner. In an attempt to lose her pursuers, the *Diligence* slips through the various banks, or shallows, where fog hangs thick and fleets of fishing boats haul in cod. But the sharp-eyed Americans gain steadily, forcing the *Diligence* north and east at a breakneck fourteen knots until the chase reaches an abrupt conclusion in icy waters.

Returning to Portsmouth after a voyage that also took Aubrey and Maturin to the Far East and back (beginning in book 5, *Desolation Island*), Aubrey proceeds immediately to Ashgrove Cottage, in Hampshire, where he is reunited with Sophie and his three young children, who do not recognize him at first. In the meantime, Maturin and

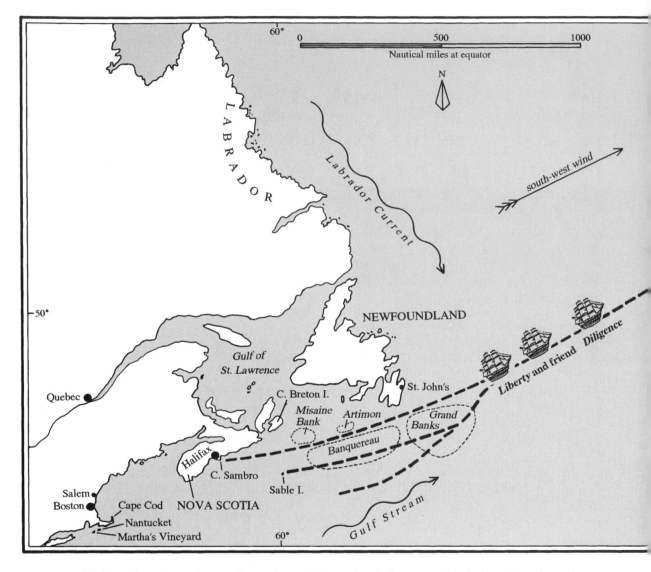

With two American privateers hot on her tail, the packet *Diligence*, carrying Aubrey, Maturin, and news of the *Shannon* victory, races home.

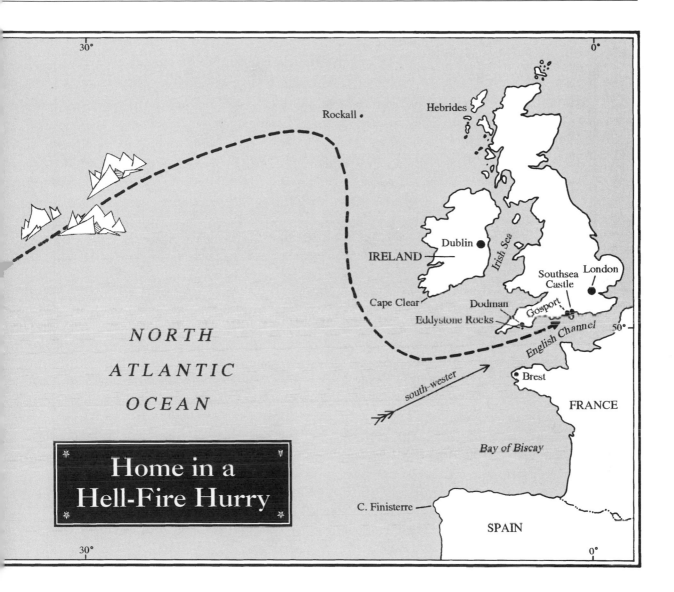

NEXT PAGE: Piloting the tricky fjords and channels between the North and Baltic seas, Aubrey delivers Maturin to the Catalan stronghold of Grimsholm.

NORWAY

NORTH
SEA

Ariel

Skager Rack

Jammer Bay

The Skaw

● Gothenburg

● Kungsbacka

SWE

Lesso I.

Cattegat

JUTLAND

Aarhus ●

The Kullen

● Helsingborg

Elsinore

D E N M

FUNEN

A R K

Great Belt

Copenhagen ●

ZEALAND

● Saltholm

● Falsterbo

North Frisian Is.

Spodsbjerg
Langelands Belt

Ariel
leads convoy

── RUGEN

Fehmarn Channel

Heligoland Bight

Pomeranian
Bay

Hamburg ●

0   50   100   150

Nautical miles

58°

56°

54°

8°

12°

12°

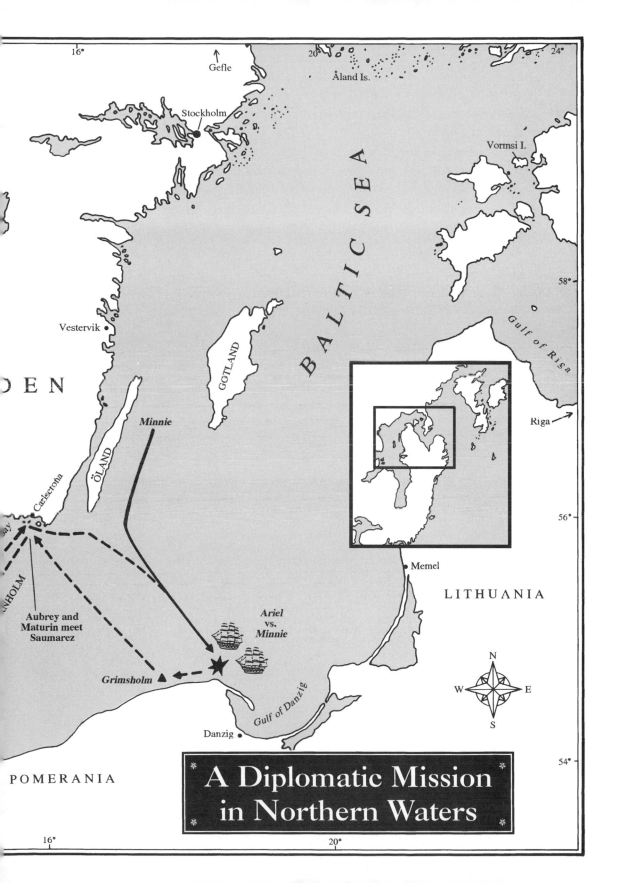

16°

Gefle

Åland Is.

Stockholm

Vormsi I.

BALTIC SEA

58°

Gulf of Riga

Vestervik

GOTLAND

Minnie

ÖLAND

Carlscrona

Riga

Bay

56°

NHOLM

Aubrey and
Maturin meet
Saumarez

Memel

LITHUANIA

Ariel
vs.
Minnie

Grimsholm

Gulf of Danzig

N

W   E

S

Danzig

54°

POMERANIA

A Diplomatic Mission
in Northern Waters

16°

20°

Villiers journey to Paris, where Maturin delivers a less-than-riveting lecture on, among other things, the extinct avifauna of Rodriguez (where he gathered specimens in book 4, *The Mauritius Command*).

Maturin leaves Villiers in France and returns to England to lay the groundwork for what he hopes will be a bloodless coup in the Baltic Sea, where his unique influence has suddenly become a potentially crucial diplomatic tool for Britain. Catalan troops are defending the fictional Baltic island Grimsholm for the French, and Maturin believes he may be able to subvert their loyalty to Napoleon. When he learns that the new Catalan commander on the island is none other than Colonel Ramon d'Ullastret i Casademon, his dashing, headstrong godfather, he becomes even more sanguine about his chances. Convincing his Whitehall allies that he can broker d'Ullastret's surrender, Maturin arranges to have Aubrey deliver him to the strategic Baltic island.

On board the sloop *Ariel* and accompanied by a young Lithuanian adviser named Jagiello, they cross the North Sea and navigate the narrow passages of the Baltic Sea (see the map "A Diplomatic Mission in Northern Waters"). Provisioning at Gothenburg, Sweden, on such exotica as smoked reindeer tongue and salted honey-buzzard and avoiding salvos from the battery at Elsinore, a fortified Danish city on the narrowest part of the sound, the *Ariel* arrives at the Swedish naval base in Carlscrona to receive additional supplies and intelligence from the nonfictional Sir James Saumarez, Vice-Admiral of the Red. In need of a second ship, Aubrey chases and captures the *Minnie*, a speedy 14-gun Danish merchantman, which Maturin then uses to penetrate the Grimsholm harbor. Here he employs his power of persuasion and strict notions of honor to their best effect.

Bound for home, the *Ariel* escorts several soldier-filled transports and a convoy of almost eight hundred merchant vessels through more tight Baltic stretches—the Fehmarn Channel, the Langelands Belt, the Great Belt—back into the Cattegat, a wide body of water separating the Baltic and North seas. Here, a north wind threatens to lay them by the lee; however, it is not this but another, more southerly, lee shore that concludes this voyage.

As Aubrey leads the transports to Santander, Spain, in the Bay of Biscay, the winds play against the *Ariel* constantly, finally driving her on the rocks—and into the hands of the French—on the Brittany coast, at the bay's northern tip. Aubrey, Maturin, and Jagiello are initially held as prisoners in a former nunnery near Brest, France, then transferred to a lonely tower in the Temple, a Revolutionary state prison in Paris. Here they plot their escape and return to England.

A view of the Tower of the Temple, the Revolutionary State Prison at Paris. Built in 1200 as part of the residence of the Templars (the most ancient of the military orders of knighthood, instituted at Jerusalem in 1118), the great tower of the Temple, flanked by four turrets, more recently served as a prison for Louis XVI, who was confined there with his family on August 13, 1792. In this tower the Dauphin, son of Louis XVI, died some months after his father. It may truly be denominated the Bastille of the revolution. We understand, however, that during the latter part of Napoleon's reign, the entire demolition of this dungeon was ordered, and we believe commenced; but we do not possess any distinct information as to the progress of that measure. (Art: Fall 1815 edition of *The Naval Chronicle*, p. 496. Text: Fall 1816 edition of *The Naval Chronicle*, p. 316.)

HERE AND THERE

Baltic Sea

An arm of the North Atlantic Ocean separating the Scandinavian peninsula from the rest of continental Europe. Bounded by Sweden, Finland, Russia, the Baltic States, Poland, Germany, and Denmark, the Baltic is connected to the North Sea by three narrow passages—the Sound, the Great Belt, and the Little Belt—leading into the Cattegat and Skagerrak (or Skager Rack) straits. Fed by many rivers, it is a shallow sea without any significant tide, and it is plagued by ice during much of the winter. With its many major ports, the Baltic has been important in trade and commerce since the Middle Ages.

Brest

A seaport on the Finistère peninsula, in the region of Brittany in northwestern France. Recognizing the advantages of Brest's sheltered harbor, Cardinal Richelieu established

A view of the Sound from above Elsinore, with Cronenburg Castle. Every nautical reader is aware, that the Sound, or as the Dutch call it, Ore Sunn, is a strait, or narrow, sea, between Denmark and Sweden through which vessels pass in going between the North Sea and the Baltic. Stretching 50 miles from northwest to southeast, the strait is about 15 miles across at its widest, but between Elsinore and Cronenburg [or Kronborg in Danish], it is not above a league wide. On passing the Sound, all ships of whatever nation or description pay a toll to the King of Denmark.

Until the Baltic expedition of 1801, when Lord Nelson dissolved the Northern Confederacy before the walls of Copenhagen, it had been the strong opinion in Europe that Cronenburg Castle, a strongly fortified royal palace, gave the Danes an unquestionable command of the passage of the Sound. That opinion has, of course, ceased to prevail.

In the distance of this view appears the town of Elsinore (Helsingør to the Danes) on the east coast of the Island of Zealand, near the mouth of the Sound and opposite to the Swedish town of Helsingborg. Towards the front of the picture is a large Dutch merchantman, and in the center is Cronenburg Castle. The English frigate (to the right), having come to an anchor off the Castle, is in the act, as is customary, of lowering her sails and firing a salute. (Spring 1807 edition of *The Naval Chronicle*, p. 393.)

a naval base there in 1631, which was fortified by the French military engineer Sébastien Vauban in the 1680s. The main base for France's Atlantic fleets during the eighteenth century, Brest played a major role in the Napoleonic wars. The British maintained a long and arduous blockade of the port, which was the planned departure point for an 1805 invasion of England that never materialized.

Elsinore or Helsingør

A seaport on the northeastern tip of Zealand, the largest island in Denmark. Its sixteenth-century Kronborg Castle was the setting for Shakespeare's *Hamlet*.

A view of the harbor of Halifax, Nova Scotia. Halifax, a town of Nova Scotia in North America, is commodiously situated on Chebucto Bay, 789 miles northeast of New York. The harbor, of which we have presented an accurate view, is a fine one, with safe anchorage, and large enough to shelter a squadron of ships throughout winter. The building of Halifax began in 1749, at which time 3,000 families were transported from England, at the expense of government, to form a settlement. Its name derives from the Earl of Halifax, to whose knowledge, care, and attention, the infant settlement was particularly indebted. The town is protected by an entrenchment and forts constructed chiefly of timber. From its situation, which is exceedingly convenient for the fishery, and from its having a communication with most parts of the province, either by hand-carriage, the sea, or navigable rivers, Halifax now enjoys a very considerable trade. The climate is healthful, but somewhat subject to fogs; winter is long and cold and summer intensely hot. (Fall 1803 edition of *The Naval Chronicle*, p. 295.)

Gothenburg or Göteborg

A seaport in southwestern Sweden, on the Göta River near where it empties into the Cattegat. The city was founded in 1619 by King Gustav II Adolph and prospered as a port, especially during the Napoleonic wars, when many other European ports were blockaded by France.

Halifax

An Atlantic seaport on the south shore of Nova Scotia, Canada. The city occupies a rocky peninsula that protrudes into Halifax Harbour—which remains ice-free throughout the year—and divides it into an inner and outer basin. Explored by Samuel de Champlain about 1605, the site was occupied in the early eighteenth century by a French fishing station. In 1749 Edward Cornwallis established a heavily fortified military base there as a rival to Louisbourg, the French stronghold in Cape Breton, naming it after the second earl of Halifax. Halifax was made the capital of Nova Scotia in 1750 and served as an important British army and navy base—one of the most heavily fortified outside Europe—until 1906.

North Sea

An arm of the Atlantic Ocean extending between continental Europe and the British Isles. With its various currents and shallow depth, the sea is unusually turbulent and subject to frequent storms. Its waters—especially the vast shallows called Dogger Banks off northern England—have long been an important source of fish for Britain and northern Europe. The North Sea has always played a crucial role in the defense of Britain and has been the site of countless sea battles over the centuries.

Sable Island

A slowly sinking sandbar in the North Atlantic Ocean, about 185 miles southeast of Halifax, Nova Scotia. The island first appeared on maps in 1544. Called the "graveyard of the Atlantic," it has been the site of numerous shipwrecks over the years.

Toil and Trouble
in the Mediterranean

The Ionian Mission opens in London, where Maturin stays at his usual lodgings, The Grapes. His new bride, Diana Villiers, meanwhile, sets up a more tradition- ally domestic household on Half Moon Street, a short walk away. Without informing her about the details—marriage has failed to relax his sense of confidentiality—Maturin travels to Portsmouth to meet Aubrey, who is now in command of an old 74-gun ship of the line, the *Worcester.*

Outward-bound to join the Toulon blockade, the *Worcester* stops in Hamoaze, a sheltered, deepwater estuary where the Plymouth Naval Base and Devonport dockyard are situated, to press sailors; and there Aubrey buys colored gunpowder to train his crew. "I have laid in a fine stock of private powder," he tells Maturin, "the stock of a fireworks maker lately deceased, a most prodigious bargain." However, before it can be spent entirely in practice, this powder makes a decidedly pyrotechnical appearance in a skir- mish between the *Worcester* and the *Jemmapes,* a taut French seventy-four, near Lorient, a maritime town in western France. No deaths result from the fighting, but Maturin manages to "cop it," as several showy but superficial wounds lay him up until the *Worcester* passes Cape St. Vincent, the southwesternmost tip of Portugal.

The *Worcester* continues on to the waters off Toulon, where the Mediterranean fleet, commanded by Admiral Thornton, is engaged in the "everlasting" blockade of this well-protected harbor in southeastern France, which for centuries has served as France's principal naval base. Due to the rigors of the blockade and the stress of nego-

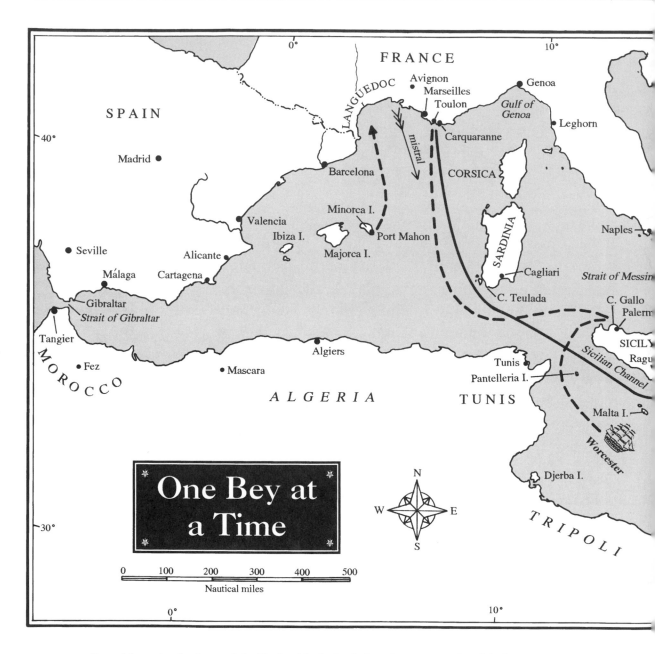

Spared from the drudgery of the Toulon blockade, Aubrey is sent on various Mediterranean missions, including one to the Ionian Islands, where he must choose an ally from among several feuding rulers.

tiating with the fickle rulers of the eastern Mediterranean—an almost inconceivable confusion of beys, pashas, sultans, and the like—Admiral Thornton is absent from the flagship's quarterdeck. Unfortunately for Aubrey, he thus falls within the power of Admiral Harte, Thornton's second in command and an acrimonious cuckold, thanks in part to Aubrey.

The Bay of Toulon. France's only naval arsenal in the Mediterranean, Toulon has 20,000 inhabitants chiefly employed in the business of the fleet. This celebrated city is divided into old and new quarters. The harbor, respecting these, is distinguished by the names of the Old Port, or Merchants' Port, and the New Port, or King's Port (the latter appellation is indeed lately abolished). The Merchants' Haven is protected by two moles, begun by Henry IV: a noble quay extends along it, on which stands the Town House. In front of this haven is an arsenal with everything requisite for constructing and fitting out vessels.

The New Haven, or King's Port, was constructed by Louis XIV, as were the city's fortifications. In front of this haven is an arsenal with naval stores, docks, and yards. The first object that catches the attention is a rope walk, entirely arched, extending as far as the eye can reach. Above is a place for the preparation of hemp. Here also is an armory for muskets, etc. In the park of artillery are cannons ranged in piles; bombs, grenades, and balls of all kinds placed in wonderful order. The long sail room, the foundry for cannon, the dock yards, basins, etc., are all well worthy of observation. The largest ships in the French Navy are built and stationed here.

The Bay of Toulon is formed on the south by a peninsula, joined to the main by a narrow low neck of land; the outer point of this peninsula is Cape Cepet. The outer or great road of Toulon is bounded by the peninsula on the south: its entrance, about a mile-and-a-half broad, is defended by many forts on both shores. The inner road is a fine basin, entered between two promontories a quarter of a mile from each other and both covered with batteries. The town is impregnable from the sea and is esteemed at all seasons the most secure in Europe. (Fall 1815 edition of *The Naval Chronicle*, p. 384.)

The *Worcester* falls into the blockade's monotonous cycle until Admiral Harte orders her, with the *Dryad*, under Captain William Babbington, to sail to Palermo. They are to rendezvous there with the armed transport *Polyphemus* and pick up a consul and gifts to be delivered to the pasha of Barka, a fictional island in the eastern Mediterranean. En route to Barka, as previously ordered by Harte, the *Dryad* sails into the port of Medina to deliver dispatches.

The *Dryad* returns to the *Worcester*, waiting offshore, bearing news that a French seventy-four and a 36-gun frigate are moored in Medina's harbor. But the laws of neutrality and Aubrey's interpretation of Harte's ambiguous orders prevent him from firing on the French vessels, an action that could have had grave ramifications. At a subsequent debriefing, Admiral Thornton, in an accusatory diatribe, insinuates that Aubrey disobeyed his orders, which, unbeknownst to him, were to sacrifice the *Dryad*, with his good friend Babbington on board, to the French at Medina in order to further Britain's strategic goals in the area.

Somewhat shaken by this unsavory episode, Aubrey sails to Port Mahon, Minorca, which has been back in the hands of the Spanish since 1802. Aubrey observes his former stomping ground and notes the transformation: "The Spanish flag rather than the Union flew over various public buildings, and now the Spanish men-of-war in the harbour were not prizes to the Royal Navy but allies, yet upon the whole little had altered."

Back on board the *Worcester*, Maturin receives word that an important, clandestine meeting that he has been trying to orchestrate with French Royalists has been confirmed for a site in Languedoc. He persuades Aubrey to deliver him to their untoward meeting place—the mouth of the marshy Aigouille River in southern France. Maturin's meeting fails to come off as planned, however, and Aubrey narrowly avoids disaster when the rickety *Worcester* encounters French men-of-war and severe weather. The *Worcester* limps back to the Toulon blockade.

The Ionian Mission concludes with another eastward voyage in the Mediterranean. After the captain of the *Surprise* is killed in action, Aubrey resumes command of his beloved former ship, a nimble if diminutive 28-gun frigate. He is ordered to proceed to the Ionian Sea, off the west coast of Greece. Accompanied again by Babbington in the *Dryad* and two transports with guns from Valletta, Aubrey must choose an ally from among three feuding rulers in the Ionian Islands, whose normally contentious relationships have been greatly exacerbated by the wars. Their destinations in this region are fictional, but Kutali and Marga would be located on the mainland near the island of Corfu, about a day's ride from Ioannina, in the Epirus Mountains.

HERE AND THERE

Barbary States

A group of independent Muslim states—Algeria, Tunisia, Tripoli, and Morocco—located along the coast of North Africa. The Barbary States were infamous as a base of piracy against European—and later U.S.—shipping in the Mediterranean from the sixteenth to the nineteenth centuries. The booty the pirates seized and the tributes they collected were the major source of income for local rulers, who also took Christian slaves. Efforts to end the attacks included the U.S. war against Tripoli (1801 to 1805), a U.S. attack on Algiers in 1815, and the bombardment of Algiers by an Anglo-Dutch fleet in 1816, but piracy was not effectively ended until the French conquest of Algeria in 1830.

Cape St. Vincent

A promontory on the Atlantic Ocean at the southwest extremity of Portugal. Near the cape, at Sagres, the prince of Portugal, Henry the Navigator, established a naval observatory and a school of navigation in 1420. Most notable of the naval battles fought off Cape St. Vincent was one in 1797 in which Admiral John Jervis, with the help of Nelson, defeated a numerically superior Spanish fleet. For their leadership in the victory, Jervis was made earl of St. Vincent and Nelson was knighted.

Ionian Isles

A group of seven islands in the Ionian Sea: Corfu, Paxos, Leucas (also called Santa Maura), Ithaca, Cephalonia, Zante, and Cythera. The islands were awarded to France in 1797 when the Venetian Republic fell. They were taken by Russo-Turkish forces two years later, only to be reclaimed by Napoleon in 1807. The Treaty of Paris in 1815 made them a protectorate of Great Britain.

Lorient

A seaport and naval base on the Bay of Biscay in Brittany, France. Originally the fortified town of Port-Louis, the seaport burgeoned when the French East India Company (Compagnie des Indes Orientale) based itself there in 1664.

Palermo

A seaport on Sicily's northwestern coast at the head of the Bay of Palermo. Founded by the Phoenicians, Palermo has been settled and ruled by many peoples. The Bourbon house of Naples controlled Palermo from 1734 until 1860.

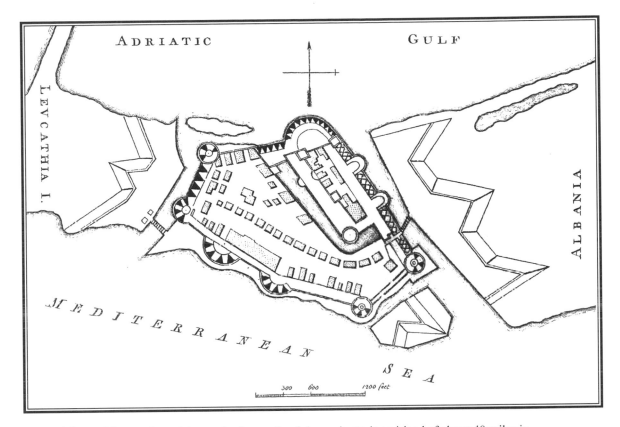

Plan of Santa Maura. Santa Maura, the Leucadia of the ancients, is an island of about 48 miles in circumference in the Ionian Sea between Corfu and Cephalonia. It was once united to the coast of Epirus, or Achia, by an isthmus, which was cut through by either the Carthaginians or the Corinthians. Today, the island is divided from the continent by a channel of about 50 paces wide. Santa Maura surrendered to the British on the 16th of April, in the present year (1810). (Spring 1810 edition of *The Naval Chronicle*, p. 153.)

Fiasco in
the Middle East

At the opening of *Treason's Harbour,* Aubrey and Maturin find themselves stranded on the island of Malta, in the central Mediterranean about sixty miles south of Sicily. A base for British ships on the Toulon blockade, Valletta's Grand Harbour bustles with naval activity. Once again Aubrey is vying with the many other captains who, for one reason or another, are temporarily without a quarterdeck to pace. Both of Aubrey's recent commands, the *Worcester* and the *Surprise,* are in port licking their wounds, the former having nearly sunk in a storm and the latter recently worked over by Turkish warships.

Admiral Sir John Thornton has died, and Sir Francis Ives is poised to take command of Mediterranean operations, which include both espionage and the blockade of the Toulon harbor, where some twenty-one French ships of the line are bottled up. In the meantime, however, Rear Admiral Harte is acting as commander in chief of the Mediterranean, and he is neither a champion of Aubrey nor a friend of Maturin.

Another Aubrey nemesis, Andrew Wray, the acting second secretary of the Admiralty, has arrived in Malta to deal with the tangled web of British and French agents and double agents that has established itself on the island. Maturin forms a relationship with

After sailing from Malta to Tina on board the *Dromedary,* the Surprises march overland to Suez, where they meet the *Niobe.* From there they sail into the Red Sea with Turkish troops and the Murad Bey.

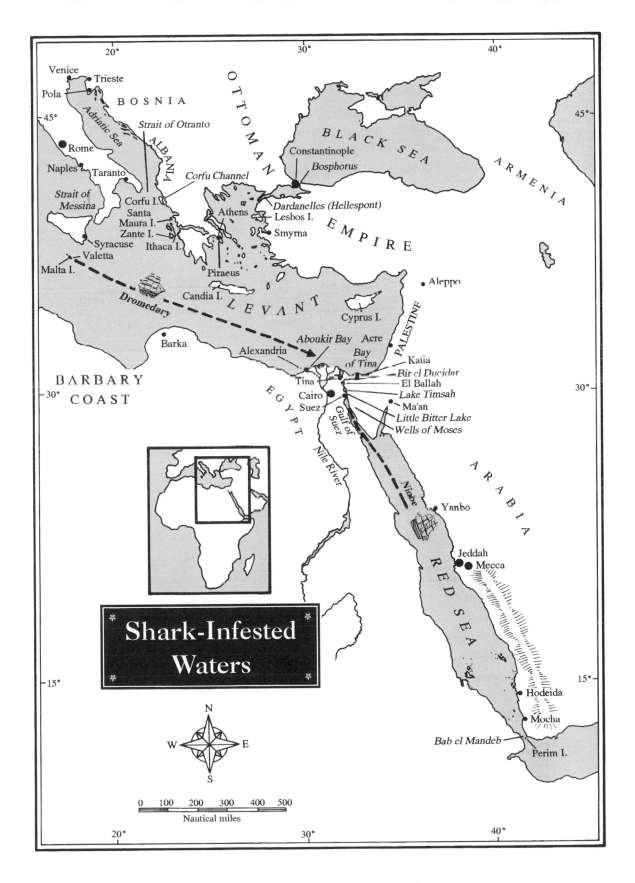

Shark-Infested Waters

Wray, a fellow music lover and an inveterate gambler. As Maturin tries to figure out the man, the ingenuous Aubrey begins to suspect that he may have been wrong to accuse the second secretary of cheating at cards years ago.

Just as Aubrey's prospects of a command start to look even dimmer—his crew is dwindling, those left are growing more dissolute daily, and commanders with greater pull are lining up ahead of him for assignment—he receives orders from Sir Francis. With Maturin and Hairabedian, an Armenian dragoman highly recommended by Wray, he is to journey to Mubara, a fictional island in the Red Sea, and with the help of Turkish troops, replace its hostile ruler with one amenable to English interests. The other purpose of his mission is to intercept a galley loaded with silver that the French plan to use to secure the favor of Mubara's ruler.

Setting out from Malta in the transport ship *Dromedary*—the *Surprise* is still being refitted and the *Worcester* has been condemned—Aubrey, Maturin, with his newfangled toy, a diving bell, and the Surprises cross the Mediterranean and land at Tina, a port in the easternmost part of Egypt on the Nile's Pelusian mouth. The Surprises, the Turkish troops, and Murad Bey, Britain's chosen leader for Mubara (picked up in Katia), travel overland from Tina to Suez, the port at the head of the Gulf of Suez. Embarking on the borrowed East India Company sloop *Niobe*, the Surprises sail down the narrow, treacherous gulf and into the Red Sea, which contains considerably fewer perils—with the notable exception of sharks.

Off Mubara, the *Niobe* encounters the supposedly treasure-laden galley, and Stephen has the opportunity to put his diving bell to what his shipmates consider gainful use. The mission is too late to achieve its diplomatic goal, and the downcast Surprises retrace their steps to Malta. There Maturin undertakes some not unpleasant counterintelligence work in the company of Laura Fielding, and Aubrey learns to his intense displeasure that the *Surprise* is to return to England to be laid up or sold out of the service.

Sir Francis gives Aubrey two quick missions to perform before taking the *Surprise* home. The first is to lead a convoy up the Adriatic to Venice. Becalmed off the island of Corfu, then under French control, the *Surprise* fends off a nighttime raid by shore boats. Aubrey's second task is to sail to the port of Zambra in Mascara, "a small but quite powerful state" in the northwestern part of what is today Algeria. Accompanied by Admiral Harte in the *Pollux*, Aubrey's job is to bolster the consul in his negotiations with the implacable dey of Mascara.

Despite the fact that "never had he felt so much one with his ship," Aubrey's Zambra mission does not come off quite as planned. Disappointed and dreading the *Surprise*'s fate, he heads for Gibraltar.

HERE AND THERE

Adriatic Sea

An arm of the Mediterranean Sea, lying between the Italian and Balkan peninsulas and linked to the Ionian Sea by the Strait of Otranto. The two shores of the Adriatic are markedly different. While the Italian coast is mostly straight and continuous, with few islands, the Balkan coastline is fragmented by inlets and dotted with many small and large islands, making navigation a complicated task. In the Middle Ages the Adriatic served as the major shipping route between Europe and the Orient, bringing much wealth to Venice, which is located at its head.

Malta

A group of islands in the Mediterranean Sea between Sicily and the northeast coast of Africa. The largest island is Malta, where the capital and chief city of Valletta is located; the other islands are Gozo, Comino, and the uninhabited rocks of Cominetto and Filfla. Because of Malta's strategic location in the Mediterranean and Valletta's magnificent deepwater harbor, the islands have been subject to numerous invasions and foreign domination. In 1530 the Holy Roman Emperor Charles V granted Malta to the powerful and wealthy Knights Hospitalers (or Knights of the Order of the Hospital of St. John of Jerusalem), a religious-military order that also became known as the Knights of Malta. The knights transformed the islands by building extensively, and Valletta's Grand Harbour grew into an almost impenetrable fortress. Nevertheless, Malta was seized in 1798 by Napoleon. After two years of blockade, Malta was captured by the British, who transformed the well-equipped dockyard built by the Knights of Malta in 1789 into their principal naval base in the Mediterranean. Britain's refusal to evacuate the island in accordance with the Treaty of Amiens was the immediate spark that led to renewed hostilities with France in 1803.

Mascara

A former state in what is now Algeria and today an Algerian city and department, also known as Mouaskar. Mascara, meaning "mother of soldiers," was founded in 1701 as a Turkish military garrison. In 1791 it was abandoned by the Spanish Muslims who had settled there and was returned to the Turks.

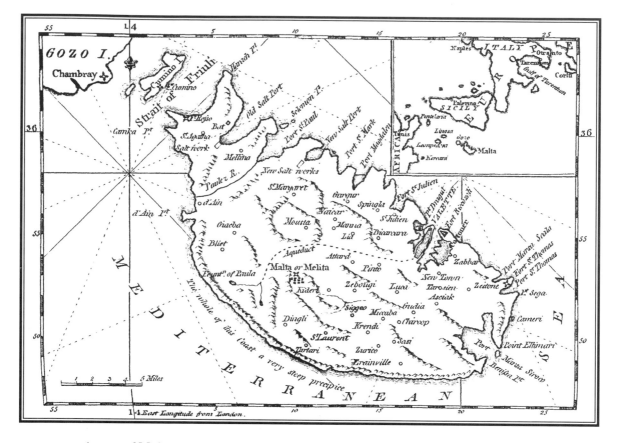

A map of Malta. "The approach of the island," reports Mr. Brydone, "is very fine although the shore is rather low and rocky. It is everywhere inaccessible to an enemy by an infinite number of fortifications. In many places, the rock has been sloped into the form of a glacis, with strong parapets and entrenchments running behind it. One side of the island is so completely fortified by nature that there was nothing left for art. The rock is of a great height and absolutely perpendicular from the sea for several miles." (Art: spring 1818 edition of *The Naval Chronicle*, 326. Text: fall 1802 edition of *The Naval Chronicle*, p. 121.)

Pelusium

An ancient Egyptian city at the eastern mouth of the Nile. Its ruins are located on the Plain of Tina. It was at Pelusium that Cleopatra and her army reentered Egypt after her brother (and husband) Ptolemy XIII expelled her in 48 B.C.

Red Sea

A long, narrow inland sea between northeastern Africa and the Arabian Peninsula. Its name comes from floating algae that from time to time give the water a reddish tinge.

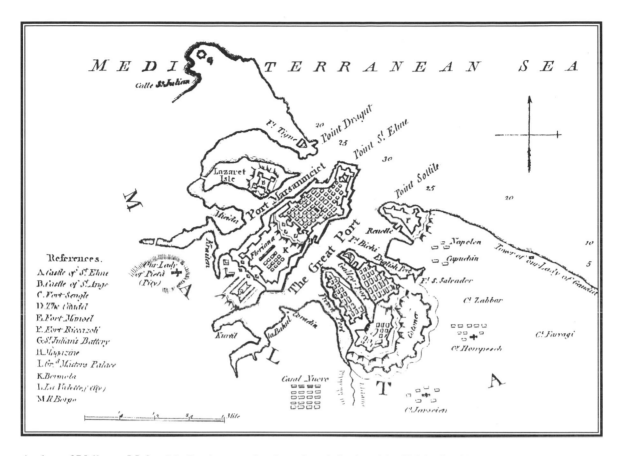

A plan of Valletta, Malta. Mr. Brydone, an "author of merit," who visited Malta in 1770, commented: "The city stands upon a peninsula, betwixt two of the finest ports in the world, which are defended by almost impregnable fortifications. That on the southeast side of the city is the largest. It runs about two miles into the heart of the island, and is so very deep and surrounded by such high grounds and fortifications that they assure us the largest ships of war might ride here in the most stormy weather, almost without a cable."

By treachery, the island fell into the hands of the French, under Bonaparte, in June 1798. After the Battle of the Nile, an English squadron appeared before Malta, and, having sustained a blockade of two years, forced the island's surrender to the British on September 5, 1800. (Map: Spring 1811 edition of *The Naval Chronicle*, p. 480. Text: Fall 1802 edition of *The Naval Chronicle*, p. 121.)

At its northern end, the Red Sea forks into the Gulf of Suez to the west and the Gulf of 'Aqaba to the east. At the southern end, the strait of Bab el Mandeb connects the Red Sea with the Gulf of Aden and the Arabian Sea.

Suez

A port city at the north end of the Gulf of Suez. First settled in ancient Egyptian times, the city's fortune has fluctuated through the centuries with the opening and closing of trade routes. Southeast of the city lie the legendary Wells of Moses, where according to the Bible, Moses fought off a group of shepherds who were attempting to drive away the seven daughters of the priest of Midian who had come to water their father's sheep.

Around the Horn
in a Hurry

Following an ill-begotten mission to the Barbary Coast at the close of book 9, *Treason's Harbour*, Aubrey and Maturin are now in Gibraltar. To Aubrey's pleasant surprise, Sir Francis Ives, commander in chief in the Mediterranean, sees fit to cast the dubious outing in a positive light, a sort of poetic justice for Aubrey, whose many victories have been downplayed or outright nabbed by self-promoting superiors. From Sir Francis, Aubrey also receives the welcome news that the *Surprise* is to remain in His Majesty's service for at least one more assignment: to intercept the American 32-gun frigate *Norfolk*, which has been dispatched from Boston to harass English whalers in the Pacific. (Although the *Norfolk* is fictional, her voyage has similarities with that of USS *Essex*, a 32-gun frigate commanded by David Porter, which made the U.S. Navy's first voyage to the Pacific between 1812 and 1815.)

There is not a moment to lose, because the *Surprise* hopes to catch the *Norfolk* before she can reach the Pacific, where finding her among the vast expanses and many uncharted islands will be far more difficult. Not far from the Cape Verde Islands, off the coast of northern Africa, the *Surprise* comes across three northbound Indiamen, and one of the company's captains tells Aubrey that he has never seen such a wide zone of calms and variables between the southeast and northeast trades. Aubrey decides to save time and forgo watering at the Cape Verdes, instead counting on collecting rainwater from the frequent storms between 9° and 3° north of the line.

A view of Gibraltar from the west. The immense base or rock at the foot of which stands the town of Gibraltar is of a singular shape and appearance much better conveyed by this view of its western front than by description. It is upwards of 1,300 feet in height and extends into the sea for a considerable length. Being connected with the continent by a low isthmus, it is believed by many to have been once wholly surrounded by the sea. The rock, at the foot of which lies the fortress of Gibraltar, is so nearly perpendicular on the Mediterranean side that all artificial modes of defense there are totally unnecessary. The western front is less precipitous, but here human ingenuity has been exerted in order to render it, if possible, impregnable.

Few situations, perhaps, in the whole world have been so peculiarly adapted by nature to withstand an attack. On the sea, an extremely dangerous shoal of rocks extends far into the bay along the western front and totally secures the fortress from the near approach of ships. The channel by which a ship may enter is extremely narrow and difficult, so that, although a ship of the line may actually heave down at the New Mole, the batteries prevent a hostile approach.

Although the barrenness of the rock might forbid the traveler from settling there as a pleasant retreat, the climate is peculiarly wholesome. During the summer, the heat is so considerably moderated by a constant sea-breeze that diseases frequently attendant on hot countries are totally unknown here. On the other hand, though the mountains in Spain and Africa are often covered with snow, it seldom falls in Gibraltar; In December and January, heavy rains and violent thunderstorms frequently occur, but they are short-lived and prove to be of only the slightest inconvenience.

In this view, a bomb-ketch, of the old construction, is introduced in the foreground, while the fleet under the command of Admiral Sir George Rooke [1650–1709], stands into the bay. (Fall 1800 edition of *The Naval Chronicle*, p. 380.)

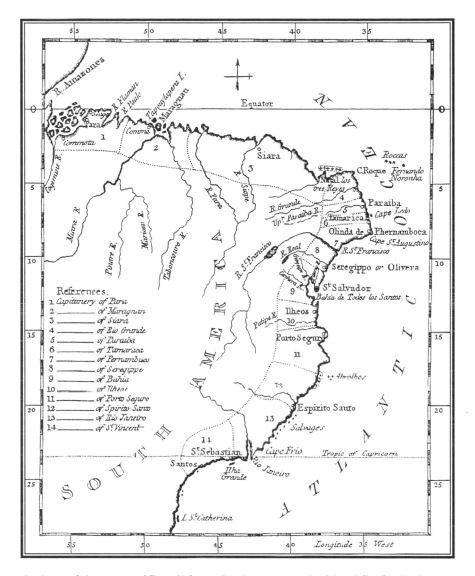

A chart of the coast of Brazil from the Amazon to the island St. Catherina. Although Brazil possesses several good harbors, St. Salvador in All Saints Bay and St. Sebastian in Rio Janeiro are the only two ports frequented by our outward-bound East India ships. They are the most capacious and convenient and the most abundant in refreshments. And at these two the narrow colonial policy of Portugal does not pose so many difficulties to access and intercourse as it does at minor stations. (Spring 1814 edition of *The Naval Chronicle*, p. 488.)

NEXT PAGE: Sent to protect the British whaling fleet in the South Pacific, the *Surprise* pursues USS *Norfolk* around Cape Horn, up the western coast of South America, and west toward the Marquesas Islands.

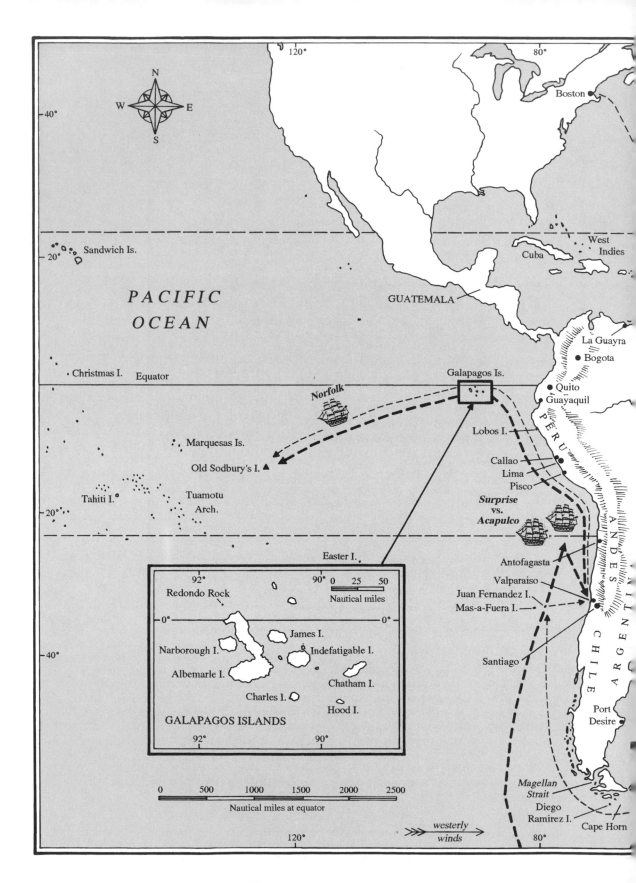

120°   80°

Boston

PACIFIC
OCEAN

20°   Sandwich Is.

GUATEMALA

West
Indies

Cuba

La Guayra
Bogota

Christmas I.   Equator   Galapagos Is.   Quito
                                                                Guayaquil

                                    Norfolk   Lobos I.

                                                                Callao
                    Marquesas Is.   Lima
            Old Sodbury's I. ▲   Pisco

Tahiti I.   Tuamotu   *Surprise*
                    Arch.   vs.
20°   *Acapulco*

                                                                Antofagasta

                                    Easter I.   Valparaiso
                                                                Juan Fernandez I.
                                                                Mas-a-Fuera I.

            92°   90°   0   25   50
        Redondo Rock   Nautical miles
40°
        0°   0°   Santiago
                            James I.
    Narborough I.   Indefatigable I.
        Albemarle I.
                                Chatham I.
                                                                Port
            Charles I.   Desire
                        Hood I.

        GALAPAGOS ISLANDS

            92°   90°

                                                                *Magellan
                                                                Strait*
    0   500   1000   1500   2000   2500   Diego
                                                                Ramirez I.
            Nautical miles at equator   Cape Horn

                                            *westerly
                                            winds*
                120°   80°

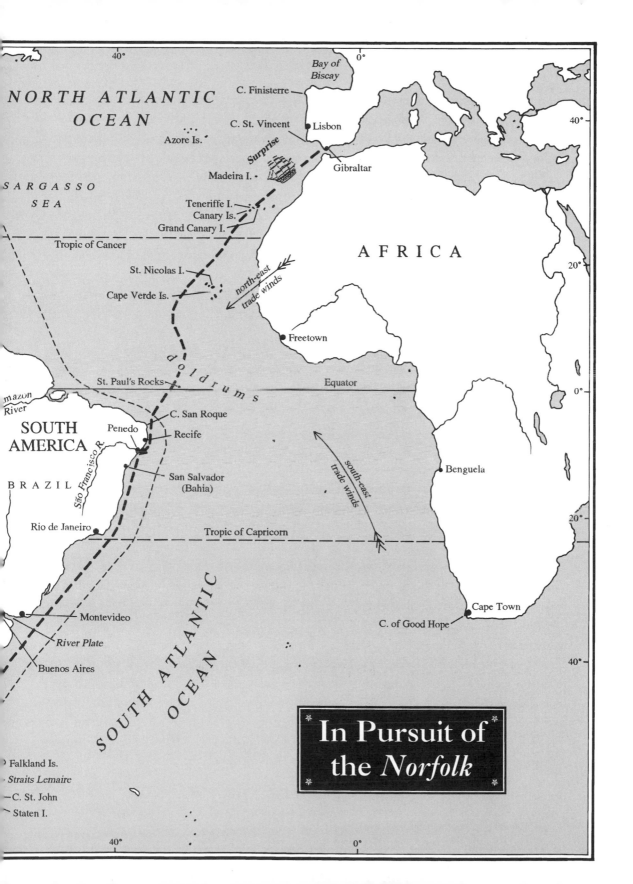

North Atlantic Ocean

Bay of Biscay

C. Finisterre

North Atlantic Ocean

C. St. Vincent • Lisbon

Azore Is.

Surprise

Gibraltar

Madeira I.

Sargasso Sea

Teneriffe I.
Canary Is.
Grand Canary I.

Tropic of Cancer

Africa

St. Nicolas I.

Cape Verde Is.

north-east trade winds

Freetown

Amazon River

St. Paul's Rocks

doldrums

Equator

South America

C. San Roque

Penedo

Recife

São Francisco R.

San Salvador (Bahia)

Brazil

south-east trade winds

Benguela

Rio de Janeiro

Tropic of Capricorn

Montevideo

River Plate

Buenos Aires

Cape Town

C. of Good Hope

South Atlantic Ocean

Falkland Is.

Straits Lemaire

C. St. John

Staten I.

In Pursuit of the *Norfolk*

The weather, however, is uncooperative as far as rain is concerned and even less so when they run into an electrical storm full of St. Elmo's fire, during which the *Surprise* is struck by lightning. The Surprises stop at Penedo, in the mouth of Brazil's São Francisco River, to repair ship. While they're there, the *Norfolk* passes by. The Surprises redouble their efforts to ready the ship, but several other mishaps impede their progress. By the time they get under way, Aubrey estimates that the *Norfolk* is two thousand miles ahead of them. Nonetheless, they carry on.

Off the coast of southern Patagonia, the *Surprise* comes across the brig *Danaë*, a packet from the Cape of Good Hope that is carrying important cargo. They hope to warn her about the presence of the *Norfolk*, but she is acting strangely evasive. As it turns out, she has been captured by the Americans. The *Surprise* retakes her, and Aubrey sends her home under Tom Pullings's command, but not before learning from her prisoners that the *Norfolk* has captured two British whalers in the South Atlantic. From a homeward-bound letter written by one of the *Norfolk*'s officers, Aubrey also discovers the captain's intentions once he reaches the Pacific. Aubrey cracks on, confident of catching up with the *Norfolk* at least by the Galapagos Islands, off the northwestern coast of South America, and hopefully farther south, in the vicinity of Valparaiso, Chile.

The *Surprise* weathers a storm that rushes her down to Staten Island (Isla de los Estados). Forced by a fierce west wind south into the freezing and treacherous sixties, the *Surprise* battles brutal weather and contrary seas to round Cape Horn.

After recuperating on Juan Fernandez Island, the *Surprise* sails for the Galapagos. En route she retakes the captured whaler *Acapulco* from the Americans, which provides Aubrey with not only a valuable cargo of whale oil but also enough spars, sail, and cordage for a lengthy voyage. Aubrey learns from her unwitting captain, a nephew of the *Norfolk*'s captain, that the *Norfolk*, after cruising the whaling waters of the Galapagos, is likely to head to the island of Huahiva in the Marquesas—where Captain Palmer plans to establish a settlement. After selling the *Acapulco* to prize agents in Valparaiso, Aubrey continues north to the Galapagos.

Once again, the *Surprise* is too late. Failing to find the *Norfolk* here, she now heads west for the Marquesas Islands. But before they can reach these wondrous South Sea Islands—which have the naturalists on board in a great state of lust—they finally discover the *Norfolk* on Old Sodbury's Island. East of the Marquesas, the tiny island is a godforsaken, shark-infested haunt known almost exclusively to whalers. Here the crews of the two ships get to know each other better than either might have wished.

HERE AND THERE

Cape Horn

The southernmost point of South America, Cape Horn is a steep headland on Horn Island, part of the Tierra del Fuego Archipelago, in southern Chile. Although Sir Francis Drake sighted the cape in 1578, the Dutch navigator Willem Schouten was the first to sail around it (in 1616), and it was named for his birthplace, the town of Hoorn, in Holland. The cape is notorious for its stormy weather, and rounding it was a test of endurance and good seamanship for sailors. False Cape Horn, located thirty-five miles northwest on Isla Hoste, another of the Tierra del Fuego islands, is sometimes mistaken for Cape Horn. (One of the best American accounts of rounding the Horn during this era is found in Richard Henry Dana, Jr.'s *Two Years Before the Mast*, a chronicle of his voyage from Boston to California and back on board the brig *Pilgrim* in 1834.)

Galapagos Islands

A group of thirteen large volcanic islands and many islets in the Pacific Ocean about six hundred miles off the coast of Ecuador. Discovered by the Spanish explorer Tomás de Berlanga in 1535, the Galapagos sheltered buccaneers and whalers until 1832, when Ecuador annexed the islands and settled them. Galapagos means "tortoises" in Spanish, and the islands are famed for their unique flora and fauna, especially the giant land tortoise, the flightless cormorant, and the marine iguana.

Marquesas Islands

Part of French Polynesia, the Marquesas are fourteen small volcanic islands in the central Pacific Ocean about nine hundred miles northeast of Tahiti. The islands were discovered by the Spanish explorer Alvaro de Mendaña in 1595 and later visited by Captain James Cook in 1774. Herman Melville would describe the islands in his first novel, *Typee: A Peep at Polynesian Life*, written in 1846.

São Francisco River

A major waterway in eastern Brazil. The eighteen-hundred-mile São Francisco flows north, northeast, and east, and enters the Atlantic Ocean about 180 miles south of Recife.

Tierra del Fuego

An archipelago at the southern tip of South America, separated from the mainland by the Strait of Magellan. The area was discovered in 1520 by Ferdinand Magellan, who named it "Land of Fire." According to Sir John Barrow's *Mutiny of the Bounty*, William Bligh, captain of the *Bounty*, wrote in his log in 1788, " 'I am fortunate perhaps in seeing the Coast of Terra del Fuego at a time when it is freest of snow, however I cannot help remarking that at this time it has not shewn itself with all the horrors mentioned by former Navigators' " (p. 41). The weather was bad enough, however, to force Bligh to abandon his plan of rounding Cape Horn and to head instead for the Cape of Good Hope.

Valparaiso

The principal seaport of Chile, about seventy-five miles northwest of Santiago on the Bay of Valparaiso. Originally a small Indian fishing village called Quintil, Valparaiso ("Valley of Paradise") was renamed in 1536 by the Spanish conquistador Juan de Saavedra after his birthplace in Spain. The city was frequently pillaged by English and Dutch pirates in the sixteenth century and was damaged by earthquakes in 1730 and 1822.

Homeward Bound from the West Indies

In *The Reverse of the Medal*, Aubrey and Maturin, on board the *Surprise*, complete the voyage to the South Seas that they began in book 10, *The Far Side of the World*. Chapter one finds them in the West Indies in the waters off Bridgetown, Barbados, where the *Surprise* is being refitted at the smallest of the three British bases in the West Indies.

Although O'Brian spends little time describing Bridgetown, it was a welcome sight to any ship's crew having been long at sea. In Captain Frederick Marryat's novel *Peter Simple*, written in 1833, Simple, a midshipman, describes Bridgetown joyfully after a long and arduous voyage from England:

> I never can forget the sensation of admiration which I felt on closing with Needham Point to enter Carlisle Bay. The beach of such a pure dazzling white, backed by the tall, green coca-nut trees . . . the dark blue of the sky, and the deeper blue of the transparent sea, occasionally varied into green as we passed by the coral rocks which threw their branches out from the bottom—the town opening to our view by degrees, houses after houses, so neat, with their green jalousies, dotting the landscape, the fort with the colours flying, troops of officers riding down, a busy population of all colours. . . . Altogether the scene realized my first ideas of Fairyland, for I thought I had never witnessed anything so beautiful. (p. 201)

While Simple was enthralled by the magical qualities of Barbados, his foremast jacks, like those of the *Surprise,* would take a keener interest in the island's more earthly pleasures, particularly its beautiful women and heavy, dark local rum.

Following the grim court-martial of several recaptured Hermiones (who mutineed in 1797), it is with heavy hearts that the Surprises finally embark for England, since their aging ship is in all likelihood headed for the breaker's yard. Also, because of the series of misfortunes that befell them in *The Far Side of the World,* many of the crew believe that either the ship is cursed or Captain Aubrey has lost his luck, at least for the moment. Still, they have received intelligence that they might cross paths with the *Spartan,* a pesky privateer from New Bedford, Massachusetts, that has been menacing British merchant ships in the Azores. They hope to intercept it before it reaches those islands.

The map "Three Spartans" (opposite) shows the *Surprise*'s route back to home waters while pursuing the *Spartan.* The *Surprise* passes through the western tip of the Sargasso Sea just north of the Tropic of Cancer, the Sargasso lying "rather more eastward than usual that year."

O'Brian's account of the homeward voyage and pursuit of the *Spartan* fills a little more than the first third of *The Reverse of the Medal.* The remainder of the book takes place in England and particularly in London. Many of these sites can be located on the maps on pages 36–37 (Southern England) and 40–41 (London).

HERE AND THERE

Azores

In the North Atlantic, this group of nine volcanic islands plus the Formigas rocks are approximately eight hundred miles from the coast of Portugal and sixteen hundred miles from North America. The Azores, also sometimes called the Western Isles, were settled by the Portuguese beginning in 1427 and became known as the crossroads of the Atlantic. Ships outbound from Europe to North America caught the easterlies south of the Azores and those returning to Europe caught the westerlies north of the island group.

From west to east the Azorean islands are Flores, Corvo, Fayal, Pico, Saint George, Graciosa, Terceira, Saint Michael (the largest and most populous), and Saint Mary. They cover an expanse of about four hundred miles between 37° and 39°N latitude, and all

❊ Three Spartans ❊

Bound for England from Barbados on the final leg of a two-book journey that took them to the South Pacific and back, the Surprises hunt for the American privateer *Spartan*, which they expect to find near the Azores.

but Saint Mary are volcanic, having steep slopes with lava cliffs and rocky shores. At 7,713 feet, Pico Alto on the island of Pico is the highest point.

Easy to find and surrounded by very deep water, the Azores offered ships an accessible destination for rest and resupply. The islands' rich volcanic soil and temperate climate (partly due to the North Atlantic current, a branch of the Gulf Stream) provided a rich harvest, including bananas, oranges, tea, and grapes, as well as ample supplies of sardines and tuna from the surrounding waters.

With richly laden merchant and treasure ships calling on Azorean ports on return trips from the Americas as well as from the Orient, the waters surrounding these islands also became a favorite hunting ground of pirates, privateers, and enemy navies. This hazard, combined with hurricanes, heavy gales, and rough North Atlantic oceans during winter, caused many ships to perish here. Some 275 wrecks are said to rest in the depths near the island of Terceira, which contained the Azores' chief port, Angra do Heroísmo. Other chief ports were Ponta Delgada, Saint Michael, and Horta, on Fayal.

The Azores were ruled by Spain between 1580 and 1640 and served as a home port for Spanish fleets. In 1591 the British made a failed attempt to take a Spanish treasure fleet here, and a subsequent hurricane sank much of the fleet (some eighty-eight ships), including the former HMS *Revenge*, which five days earlier, under Sir Richard Grenville, had been taken by the Spanish after courageously battling fifty-three enemy ships for fifteen hours.

Barbados

The easternmost of the Windward Islands in the West Indies, Barbados was claimed by England in 1605 and settled by English colonists in 1627. A relatively flat coral and sediment island, with no good natural harbor, Barbados gained its wealth during the seventeenth and eighteenth centuries primarily from its sugarcane plantations and the export of molasses and rum. Slaves from Africa were imported to work the fields until slavery was abolished in the British Empire in 1834.

In 1814, 128 officers and men were stationed at the naval base in Bridgetown (the island's capital and chief port) to support British naval operations in the area. Larger bases were located on the islands of Jamaica (314 officers and men) and Antigua (332 officers and men).

The following description of Barbados is an edited account from the fall edition of *The Naval Chronicle* for 1817:

> This little island, which consists of something more than 100,000 acres of land, lies the furthest east and north of all our West Indian colonies and is elevated on a ridge of calcareous rock, which rises 50 feet or more above the level of the beach and forms a sort of promontory round the north-eastern part of the island. The coast, wherever I had an opportunity of observing it, is lined with white coral, and the strand is of a beautiful light and soft sand. At a distance, the land appeared extremely bare, but as we approached it more nearly, the rich and curious tropical produce captivated our eyes.

Needham's Point, Carlisle Bay, Barbados. Barbados may be seen in clear weather at the distance of nine or 10 leagues; the east side is the lowest; to the north, the land is rugged, and broken; along the southeast side, there is a ledge of rocks about a mile offshore; from Needham's Point there is a small reef with the sea breaking over it. For many leagues to the east of the island, the sea is discolored, although there are no soundings; probably this may be produced by the waters of the great river Oroonoco, if it be admitted that the strength of its stream is sufficient to reach so far to the north as 90 or 100 leagues.

Barbados must always be a very important station in the Windward Islands, as it is the most prominent point to the eastward of all our insular possessions, which lie in the form of a semicircle in the American Archipelago and consequently are most accessible from that island which is the furthest to windward.

Bridgetown, situated at the southwestern extremity of the island and named for a small bridge over an adjoining stream, is the metropolis of this small colony, where the legislature and the principal courts of justice hold their sessions and where all the foreign trade of the island is carried on. Large ships do not approach the wharfs of the town; but they are lined with boats, canoes, and negroes, all the commercial business being carried on in this quarter.

In coming ashore south of the town, you pass by the ruins of an old pier-head, demolished by the fury of the surf in the hurricane of the year 1780, which shook this island to its foundation, destroying, it is said, between 4,000 and 5,000 of its inhabitants. The wind blew with such violence, that a heavy piece of ordnance was overset on its carriage.

It is now nearly 200 years since this island was first occupied by the English. Before that time, though it had been visited and named by the Spaniards and Portuguese, it is said not to have been laid down in any sea chart. The land is so low that it may be easily passed unseen on entering the American Archipelago and is extremely difficult of access because of adverse winds and currents, which are often insurmountable to inexperienced or unskillful navigators. (p. 393)

The City
Also known as the "Square Mile," the City encompasses the oldest section of London, that part that was within the medieval city walls. It is also the location of many of the capital's primary financial institutions, including the Bank of England, Midland Bank, the Royal Exchange, the Stock Exchange, and Lloyd's Bank. Guildhall, St. Paul's Cathedral, and Fleet Street are located in the City as well. The Temple is found in the southwest corner of the City along the Thames, and the Tower of London in the south-east corner.

The Inns of Court
Established in the fourteenth century in London to promote the practice and teaching of common law, the four Inns of Court—the Inner Temple, Middle Temple, Lincoln's Inn, and Gray's Inn—were private associations that supervised legal education and controlled admission to the bar in Great Britain. To be admitted to the bar, law students had to enroll at an inn for a period of pupilage and pass an exam. Other legal societies called the Inns of Chancery performed a similar function until the nineteenth century, when they were discontinued.

Sargasso Sea
An oval-shaped area of sea in the southwest quarter of the North Atlantic Ocean, east of the Bahama Islands and west of the Azores, between 20° and 35°N latitude and 30° and 75°W longitude, named for sargassum, a type of seaweed that floats there in large patches. Covering an area roughly two-thirds the size of the contiguous United States, the Sargasso Sea is a relatively shallow and warm pool sitting on deeper, colder waters

and contained by clockwise swirling currents. To the north is the Gulf Stream and to the south the north equatorial current.

Over a period of hundreds of thousands of years, fish, crabs, shrimp, worms, and other species have adapted special qualities for living in this unique ecosystem—most notably camouflage coloring. The Sargasso Sea is the spawning ground of flying fish and the European and North American eel.

First reported by Columbus, who thought it indicated land, the Sargasso was the source of much fear by later seamen, who told highly exaggerated stories of ships trapped in the seaweed and unable to make their way out. In reality, while seaweed islands did not impede sailing ships, the lack of wind in the horse latitudes did, so the area was largely avoided. In this passage from *The Cruise of the Cachalot* (1899), Frank T. Bullen describes the Sargasso Sea during a slow passage through it on board a New Bedford whaler:

And now we were within the range of the Sargasso Weed, that mysterious *fucus* that makes the ocean look like some vast hayfield, and keeps the sea from rising, no matter how high the wind. It fell a dead calm, and the harpooners amused themselves by dredging up great masses of the weed, and turning out the many strange creatures abiding therein. What a world of wonderful life the weed is, to be sure! In it the flying fish spawn and the tiny cuttle-fish breed, both of them preparing bounteous provision for the larger denizens of the deep that have no other food. Myriads of tiny crabs and innumerable specimens of less-known shell-fish, small fish of species as yet unclassified in any work on natural history, with jelly-fish of every conceiv-

Fleet Street, looking westward, 1820, showing Temple Bar and Old Dunstan's Church. " 'And then, sir,' Prat went on, now addressing himself more to Sir Joseph, 'the postboy, having seen his fare walk off northwards up Bell Yard, wheeled his chaise down Temple Lane, called a street boy to water his horses in Fountain Court, and went back to the mutton-pie shop on the corner by Temple Bar, where the hackney-coaches stand: it is open all night' " (*The Reverse of the Medal*, p. 203).

able and inconceivable shape, form part of this great and populous country in the sea. At one haul there was brought on board a mass of flying-fish spawn, about ten pounds in weight, looking like nothing so much as a pile of ripe white currants, and clinging together in a very similar manner. (p. 28)

The Temple

Originally the Temple was the English headquarters of the crusading Order of Knights Templars, a wealthy and powerful organization founded in the twelfth century to protect pilgrims on the road to Jerusalem. Several centuries later, possession of the Temple passed to the Crown. It was occupied by two of the Inns of Court, the Inner Temple and the Middle Temple.

Temple Bar

Originally a chain between two wooden posts marking the western limit of the City of London, where the Strand meets Fleet Street. By 1351 the Temple Bar was a wooden gate topped by a prison. In the early 1670s, Christopher Wren erected a new gate of Portland stone with a central arch for carriages. From 1684 to 1746 the Temple Bar was used to display the severed heads and sometimes other body parts of traitors. In 1806 the gate was repaired and covered in black velvet for the funeral of Nelson. The Temple Bar was removed in 1877 to improve traffic flow.

Redemption in the Azores and on the Normandy Coast

After Jack Aubrey's misfortunes of book 11, *The Reverse of the Medal*, the misused captain rebounds in *The Letter of the Marque*. The novel opens with the *Surprise*, newly bought out of the service by Stephen Maturin, preparing for a quasi-official political mission to South America. Although the *Surprise* now probably has "a more efficient, more professional ship's company than any other vessel her size afloat," the only way to weed out malcontents and ne'er-do-wells before the long voyage and to meld the crew into an efficient and happy war machine is to take a cruise, work the great guns, and, with any luck, battle both harsh weather and an enemy warship, preferably one of equal or superior strength.

Embarking from the fictional town of Shelmerston, on the southwest coast of England, the *Surprise* sets out on a trial run with few provisions. However, at sea Aubrey soon discovers from the *Merlin*, an American merchant schooner, that if the *Surprise* cruises down to the Azores, she stands a good chance of polishing off some unfinished business. The *Spartan*, the American privateer that the *Surprise* chased from the Azores to European waters in *The Reverse of the Medal*, is again on the prowl. This time she plans to top off her string of prizes taken in the Azores by ambushing the *Azul*, a three-masted barque-rigged privateer carrying 150 tons of quicksilver from Cadiz, Spain, to Cartagena, on the Spanish Main.

By now Aubrey knows this expanse of ocean and isle so well that he can picture in "his mind's eye . . . a chart of the Atlantic between thirty-five and fifty degrees N, with the Azores in the middle." He calculates that the *Spartan*'s path will take it between Saint Michael's and Saint Mary, the two southern- and easternmost islands of the Azores. While their captain plots the swiftest course that wind and current will allow, the Surprises scrape together a meager batch of supplies and remake their ship into a decent approximation of the *Azul*, all the way down to her sky blue paintwork. However, despite arriving at just the desired position, the *Surprise* is too late—or so her crew thinks, until gun flashes appear on the eastern horizon.

Back in the busy streets of London, Maturin and Martin, his surgeon's mate, restock the *Surprise*'s medicine chest and bask in the glory of their new fortune. Maturin meets with Sir Joseph Blaine and exchanges information about Aubrey's action, Diana, and intelligence matters, and the groundwork is laid for a mission that will give Aubrey the opportunity to further several goals.

The *Surprise*'s next action is one more directly related to their planned mission to South America and one that, successfully accomplished, could greatly improve Aubrey's chances for reinstatement in the Navy. From Shelmerston the ship runs down "under easy sail to Polcombe," where her crew trains in an isolated cove for an attack on the harbor of the fictional port of St. Martin's, on the Channel coast of France. At St. Mar-

A view of Cadiz. The capital of Andalusia, Cadiz is shown here by Mr. Pocock from the south. (Spring 1810 edition of *The Naval Chronicle*, p. 45.)

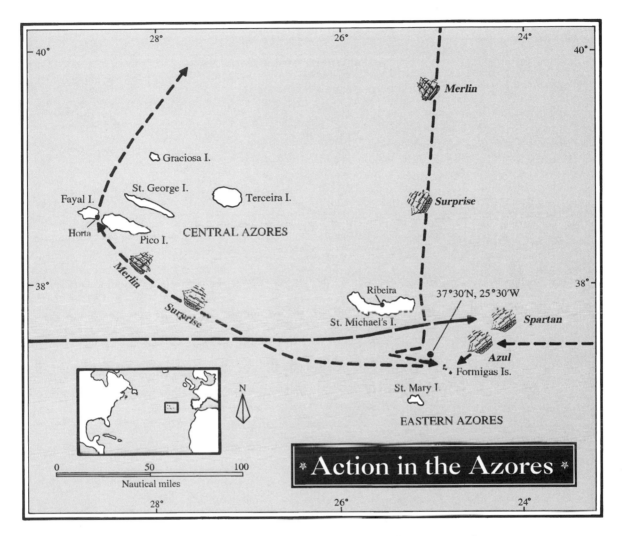

Although it was supposed to be just a quick voyage to shape up his crew, Aubrey cannot forgo a golden opportunity. When they discover that the *Spartan* is wreaking havoc in the Azores, the Suprises fly south to meet her.

tin's, which Aubrey helped the master of the *Bellerophon* chart in 1797, the plan is to cut out the thirty-gun frigate *Diane*, which, like the *Surprise*, is preparing for a high-stakes, high-pressure mission to South America.

Finally, *The Letter of Marque* takes Aubrey and Maturin to the Baltic by separate means. Maturin, who is on a personal mission to find Diana and to reconcile their relationship, plans to catch the mail packet from Leith, Scotland, a seaport and shipbuilding center now merged with Edinburgh, to Stockholm, Sweden. But instead he is

Charing Cross, 1820, looking eastward, showing Northumberland House and the Strand. "His road took him along the crowded Strand to the even more crowded Charing Cross, where at the confluence of three eager streams of traffic a cart-horse had fallen, causing a stagnation of wagons, drays and coaches round which horsemen, sedan-chairs and very light vehicles made their way among the foot passengers, while the carter sat unmoved on the animal's head, waiting until his little boy should succeed in undoing the necessary buckles" (*The Letter of Marque*, p. 113).

Piccadilly, looking westward, showing Tichborne Street and buildings removed to form Piccadilly Circus, 1820. "Sir Joseph cast up his hands, but he only said, 'Come. I will see you to the corner of Piccadilly. There is always a knot of link-boys there. Two will see you home and two will see me back' " (*The Letter of Marque*, p. 124).

offered and accepts transport aboard the *Leopard*, never an exalted ship (despite Aubrey's dramatic victory over the *Waakzaamheid* while commanding her) and now a hogged, slack transport vessel, which is bound for Gefle (Gävle), a seaport in eastern Sweden, north of Stockholm. The *Leopard*'s voyage is none too smooth, and after a fair passage down the Cattegat and through the Great Belt, the narrow channel between the Danish islands of Fyn and Sjaelland (also called Seeland or Zealand), she loses her fore-topmast north of Öland, off the east coast of Sweden, slowing her progress.

Long after Aubrey had supposed Maturin to have reached his destination, the *Surprise* catches up to the *Leopard* in the Baltic and gives the doctor a lift, both mentally and physically, to his destination. While in northern waters, Aubrey plans to call at Riga, a port in Russian-ruled Latvia, to purchase cordage, spars, and poldavy, a coarse canvas used for sail-cloth. For a map of the Baltic, see "A Diplomatic Mission in Northern Waters," pp. 106–7.

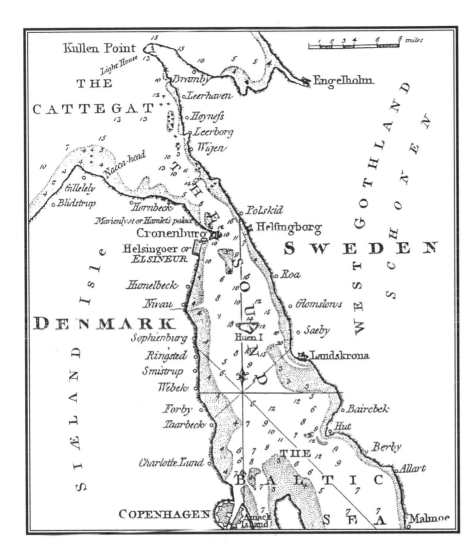

A chart of the Sound, Baltic, the Cattegat. The Oresund (Öre in Danish, or Öre in Swedish, signifies shoal or sandy shore, sund, a strait between two islands or between an island and the mainland) is the channel between the coast of Sweden and the Danish island of Zealand. The Sound's entrance from the Cattegat is between a mass of rocks on the Swedish shore named Kullen, and the northeast part of Zealand, and it terminates toward the Baltic, between Falsterbo, in Sweden, and Cape Steven in Denmark. The deepest water is on the Danish shore; the Swedish being shoal, with an increasing accumulation of sand. (Fall 1815 edition of *The Naval Chronicle*, p. 332.)

HERE AND THERE

Riga

One of czarist Russia's major seaports and now the capital of Latvia, Riga is situated near the mouth of the Western Dvina River, on the Gulf of Riga, an arm of the Baltic Sea. Like the Swedish city of Stockholm, Riga was known in the days of the square-rigged ship for the exceptional quality of its tar. Distilled from pine resin, tar was essential on board ship for the preservation of rigging and ropes.

The Beacon on Bell Rock, in the mouth of the Frith of Forth near Leith. The lighthouse on Bell Rock was originally projected by the ingenious Captain Joseph Brodie in the year 1791. Captain Brodie's many years of arduous perseverance to evince its practicality were later acknowledged by the corporation of merchants and traffickers of Leith in the presentation to that gentleman of a piece of plate. (Fall 1815 edition of *The Naval Chronicle*, p. 129.)

Shelmerston

A fictional seaport on the English Channel and home of many of the *Surprise*'s prime seamen. Shelmerston is located in the West Country (southwest England, including Avon, Cornwall, Devon, Dorset, Somerset, and Wiltshire counties), most likely in Devon, and perhaps on Torbay, with the fictional towns of Allacombe and Flicken south and south by east respectively. (See the map "Southern England," pp. 36–37.)

Serving as a home port for the letter of marque *Surprise*, Shelmerston faces east in a protected bay that "on either hand . . . curved out in tawny cliffs." As O'Brian describes the village, which is notable both for its religious fervor and the friendliness of its numerous prostitutes, it is "a curious little place, much given to smuggling, privateering, and chapel-going. There were almost as many chapels as there were public houses." Indeed, one can see the Sethians' small white marble chapel decorated with gilt brass esses from the Channel, and it makes "a striking contrast with the rest of the town, mostly thatched, homely, vague in outline."

Spanish Main

A romantic name for the Spanish possessions in America, consisting originally of the northeast coast of South America from the Isthmus of Panama to the Orinoco but by the late seventeenth century also including the Caribbean and its islands. The term was associated with the English buccaneers based in the area who would loot Spanish ships on their way back to Spain laden with treasure.

Woolcombe House

The Aubrey estate near the fictional village of Woolhampton in the county of Dorset (see map of Southern England, pp. 36–37). (Although in book 13, *The Thirteen Gun Salute*, it is implied that the estate is in Somerset, in all other cases it appears to be in Dorset; book 13 also indicates, in one instance, that Aubrey represents "Milford" at Parliament, when this should be "Milport.") While the Aubrey estate appears to be fictional, Woolcombe is not an uncommon name in Dorset. *Domesday Book*, the survey of England made in 1086, lists two: one in what is now Melbury Osmond, and another, the current Woolcombe Farm, in Toller Porcorum. The Aubreys' Woolcombe House lies in "a dank hollow, facing north." In book 7, *The Surgeon's Mate*, Jack rides through Woolhampton on his way from Woolcombe House to the town of Blandford, where he catches a post-chaise back to Hampshire. In book 17, *The Commodore*, Aubrey describes the estate his father, General Aubrey, let run to seed in his later years: "The Woolcombe Estate is nothing much—poor spewy land, most of it—but it is amazingly troublesome, with some uncommon wicked tenants, poachers to a man."

False Starts
and the East Indies

In *The Thirteen Gun Salute,* Aubrey and Maturin set out aboard the *Surprise* from Shelmerston on a voyage to South America. Ostensibly their intention is to harass French and American merchants, whalers, and fur traders, but their true, clandestine mission is to subvert Spanish hegemony and French agents in Chile and Peru. Many events, however, will intervene between the *Surprise*'s departure from England and her arrival along the shores of South America. Indeed, the circumnavigation that Aubrey and Maturin will soon embark on will take O'Brian some four books to complete.

The first distraction comes in the form of a speedy snow spied in remote waters far to the south of Cape Clear, Ireland. Convinced the snow is a potential prize, the *Surprise* chases, and the snow scurries northeast into the Irish Sea. An overnight pursuit creates a great moral dilemma for Maturin and takes the combatants so far north that the *Surprise* ultimately sails around the top of Ireland. Finally, having passed the Giant's Causeway, she weathers Malin Head, avoiding the often treacherous waters around the islands of Inishtrahull and the Garvans. She then sails well out into the open seas of the Atlantic and resumes her intended course for Lisbon, Portugal.

The *Surprise* sets out for South America and is lured into the Irish Sea by a potential prize. In Lisbon, Sir Joseph Blaine catches up with Aubrey and Maturin to deliver an urgent new assignment. They return posthaste to Portsmouth, where Aubrey takes command of the *Diane.*

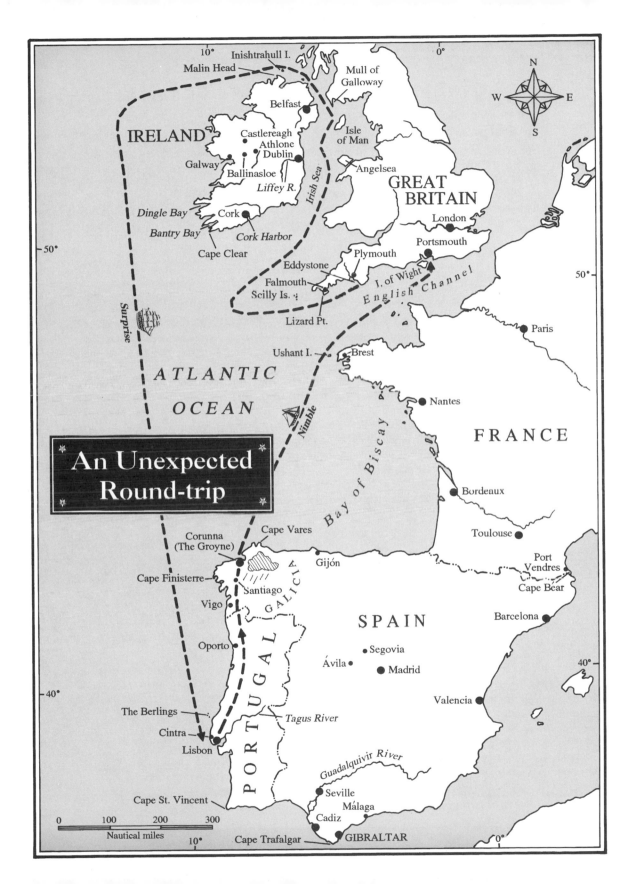

An Unexpected Round-trip

Having reached Lisbon at last, Maturin discovers from Sir Joseph Blaine, who is lodged near the town of Cintra, that his mission to South America has been betrayed to the Spanish. To save face, the *Surprise* must continue on her stated privateering cruise, but Aubrey and Maturin are to embark on an interim mission to an even more distant destination than South America. First they must return to England with Sir Joseph Blaine—by coach to Corunna, on the northern coast of Spain, and then via the cutter *Nimble* to Portsmouth. Aubrey and Maturin are to sail on board the *Diane*—the frigate they cut out of St. Martin's, France, in *The Letter of Marque*—to the South China Sea to help Mr. Fox, the king's envoy, secure a treaty of cooperation with a Malay sultanate. Blaine makes it clear that this diplomatic voyage carries significant consequences for

The Giant's Causeway on the north coast of Ireland. The Giant's Causeway, from a drawing by Mr. Pocock, is a promontory of Ireland situated in the county of Antrim, west of Bengore Head. The Causeway, strictly so denominated, is regarded as a great natural curiosity. Twiss, the celebrated tourist, thus describes it: "It consists of about 30,000 pillars, mostly in a perpendicular situation; at low water the causeway is about 600 feet long and probably runs far into the sea. . . . These kinds of columns are continued, with interruptions, for near two miles along the shore. That parcel of them which is most conspicuous and nearest the causeway the country people call the looms or organs. These pillars are just 50 in number, the tallest about 40 feet in height. . . . The others gradually decrease in length on both sides of it, like organ pipes. (Fall 1807 edition of *The Naval Chronicle*, p. 126.)

A view of the harbor at Lisbon. This Design gives a correct view of the noble harbor of Lisbon with the Castle of Belim, which during the last War (we believe in the year 1780) was nearly destroyed by Captain John Willett Payne, in the *Artois*, when the Portuguese government, allowing itself to be influenced by evil advisers, who wished to destroy the harmony existing between that country and Great Britain, threatened to sink the *Artois* and a sloop that was with her and had actually sent out some Roman Catholic Priests to anathematize the Captain. The discharge of a single gun—Captain Payne intended only to alarm them with the report of an unloaded gun, but a shot had been inserted by the sailors—from the *Artois* soon brought them to their senses. The Castle of Belim by this means lost one of its turrets, as is represented in the plate.

The View is taken by Mr. Pocock, as looking to the east, or up the Tagus. In front is one of the vessels called bean-cods, no less remarkable for swift sailing than for the singular construction. In the distance are the Spanish men of war that were taken by Sir J. Jervis in the Battle of the 14th of February off Cape St. Vincent. (Fall 1799 edition of *The Naval Chronicle*, p. 208.)

Britain, but he also tells Maturin that he might still accomplish his intentions vis-à-vis South America, approaching the goal from a different direction, as it were.

Commissioned on board the *Diane* on May 15, 1813, Aubrey and Maturin set sail with a crew of 209, including more than forty Royal Marines and Mr. Fox. To take advantage of currents and winds, Aubrey navigates a course that takes the *Diane* southwest toward Brazil, and then he heads south to the forties to catch the dependable west winds. The *Diane* touches briefly at Tristan da Cunha and avoids the Cape of Good

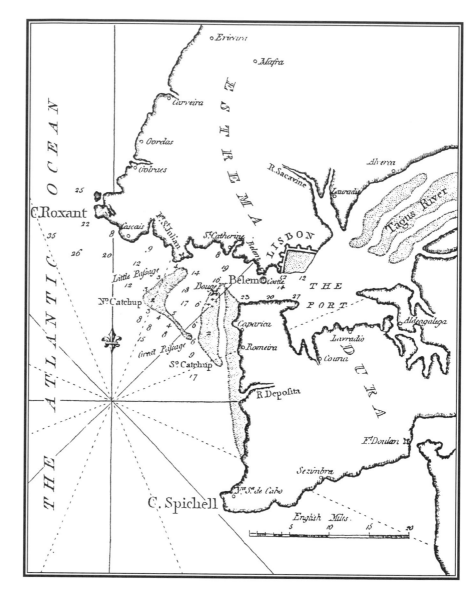

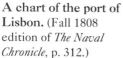

A chart of the port of Lisbon. (Fall 1808 edition of *The Naval Chronicle*, p. 312.)

Hope, which was then in the control of the British. Calling at the Cape might have meant a loss of time and possibly of hands, who would be tempted to desert at the Cape but not at the remote island of Tristan.

Much to Maturin's dismay, the *Diane* is unable to touch at Amsterdam Island as Aubrey intends to do to check his longitude and to ship fresh water. Aubrey sails the *Diane* to within five miles of the island, but she cannot stop because of contrary winds and currents.

A view of the Moorish Palace in Cintra, Portugal. Cintra, a town in the Portuguese province of Estramadura rendered memorable by a disgraceful convention between the British and French armies in the year 1808, is situated about 13 miles northwest of Lisbon. [Note: In the convention of Cintra, signed after the defeat of the French under General Andoche Juno at the battle of Vimeiro, British commanders agreed to transport the French back to France with all their arms, thus failing to eliminate a major force permanently and dampening the political benefit of the victory. In Parliament, harsh criticism of the convention and the generals resulted.] The town lies between the mountains of Cintra, anciently called the mountains of the Moon, at the mouth of the Tagus, and contains four parish churches. Its population amounts to about 1,900. The Moorish palace, of which a view is presented, was built by King Joseph, sometime before 1750. It occupies the site of a palace, actually built by the Moors, which was destroyed by an earthquake in 1655. The present edifice is in the same style of architecture as the former. (Spring 1810 edition of *The Naval Chronicle*, p. 308.)

At Java, at last, Aubrey and Maturin meet the nonfictional Thomas Stamford Raffles, who served as Java's lieutenant governor-general from 1811 to 1816 (when it was returned to the Dutch). As in *The Thirteen Gun Salute*, Raffles *was* born at sea in 1781 and was an avid naturalist. In fact, he helped found the London Zoo and served as the first president of the London Zoological Society. But certainly he never actually delivered the classic O'Brian understatement regarding the destination to which Aubrey and Maturin are to escort Fox: " 'I have never been to Pulo Prabang, alas, but I understand it possesses all the advantages of Borneo without the drawback of head-hunters.' "

A view of Amsterdam Island. Prior to the general use of chronometers and lunar observations, it was customary for ships bound to the Oriental sea to sight the islands St. Paul and Amsterdam for a correction to their longitude. The two islands are nearly on the same meridian about 17 leagues apart and may be seen from about 20 leagues in clear weather.

In 1697, the Dutch navigator Vlaming examined these islands and called the northernmost Amsterdam, and the southernmost St. Paul. The latter, which is the largest, the most accessible, and the best known, is sometimes called Amsterdam by the English. It extends northwest and southeast eight or 10 miles, and is about five miles in breadth.

On the east side of the island of St. Paul, an inlet leads to a circular basin that was the crater of a volcano, and into which the sea ebbs and flows over a causeway at the entrance of the inlet. . . . American and sometimes English vessels leave part of their crews on this island to kill seals &c. and return at fixed periods for the oil and skins procured by their people. (Fall 1813 edition of *The Naval Chronicle*, p. 321.)

Pulo Prabang, the equatorial volcanic island, is fictional. If it did exist, it would lie in the vicinity of the Lingga Archipelago. To get there, Aubrey must navigate some treacherous, piratical waters, including the narrow Banka (or "Bangka") Strait, between Banka and Sumatra. Tensions between the idle diplomats and the busy crew mount, but Aubrey maintains his intense focus on navigating the *Diane* and, using the excellent instructions and chart of the hydrographer Muffitt, carries her safely to her destination.

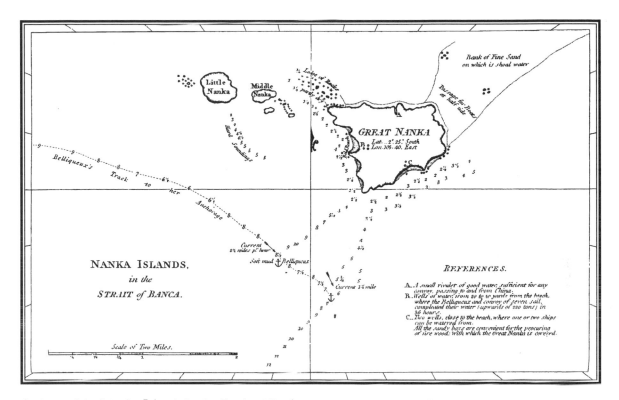

A chart of the Nanka Islands in the Strait of Banka. When the *Belliqueux* [a third-rate of 64 guns] and her convoy of seven sail passed through the Banka Strait, they stopped off at the Nanka Islands, which they charted, to procure water and firewood. (Fall 1813 edition of *The Naval Chronicle*, p. 488.)

With the accomplishment of their mission in Pulo Prabang, the Dianes head for their rendezvous with the *Surprise* off the False Natunas, named by "the master of some ship bound for the real Natunas but who was sadly out in his dead-reckoning." Losing one's way—or worse, one's ship—was not uncommon in the waters of the East Indies. To wit, this passage about the nearby Strait of Sunda, written the same year Aubrey and Maturin visited the area and taken from the spring 1815 *Naval Chronicle*, which quotes from Krusenstern's *Memoir on a Chart of the Strait of Sunda &c.* (1813): "Although a strait so important as that of Sunda, frequented every year by more than 50 European ships,

NEXT PAGE: The *Diane* escorts Fox, the king's emissary, to the equatorial island of Pulo Prabang. They sail well south of the tip of Africa, through the Sunda Strait to Batavia on the island of Java, and then north through the Banka Strait to Pulo Prabang.

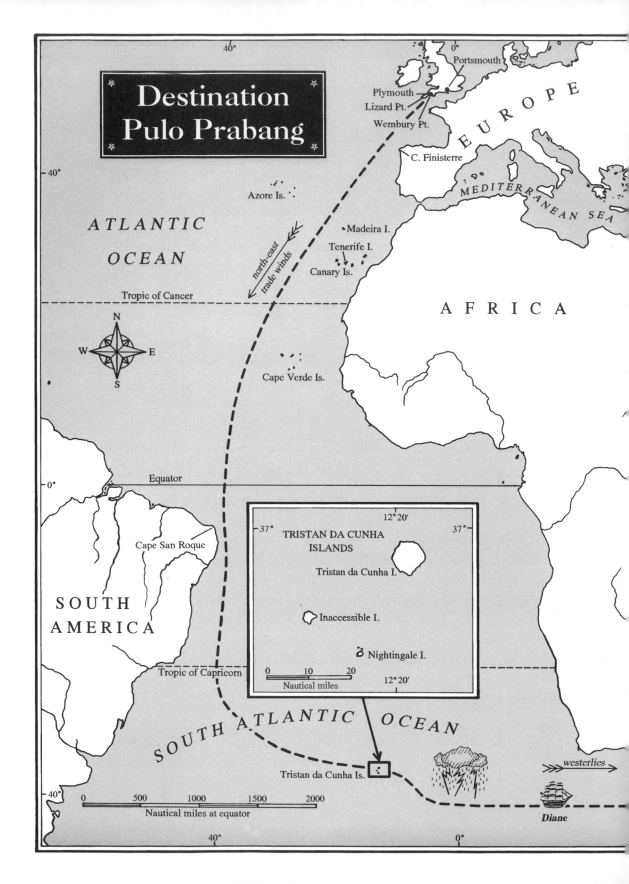

Destination
Pulo Prabang

EUROPE

Portsmouth

Plymouth
Lizard Pt.
Wembury Pt.

C. Finisterre

MEDITERRANEAN SEA

Azore Is.

Madeira I.

Tenerife I.

Canary Is.

AFRICA

ATLANTIC

OCEAN

Tropic of Cancer

north-east trade winds

N

W   E

S

Cape Verde Is.

Equator

TRISTAN DA CUNHA
ISLANDS

Tristan da Cunha I.

Cape San Roque

Inaccessible I.

Nightingale I.

SOUTH
AMERICA

Tropic of Capricorn

10   20
0
Nautical miles

12°20'

SOUTH ATLANTIC OCEAN

westerlies

Tristan da Cunha Is.

0   500   1000   1500   2000
Nautical miles at equator

Diane

40°

0°

37°

37°

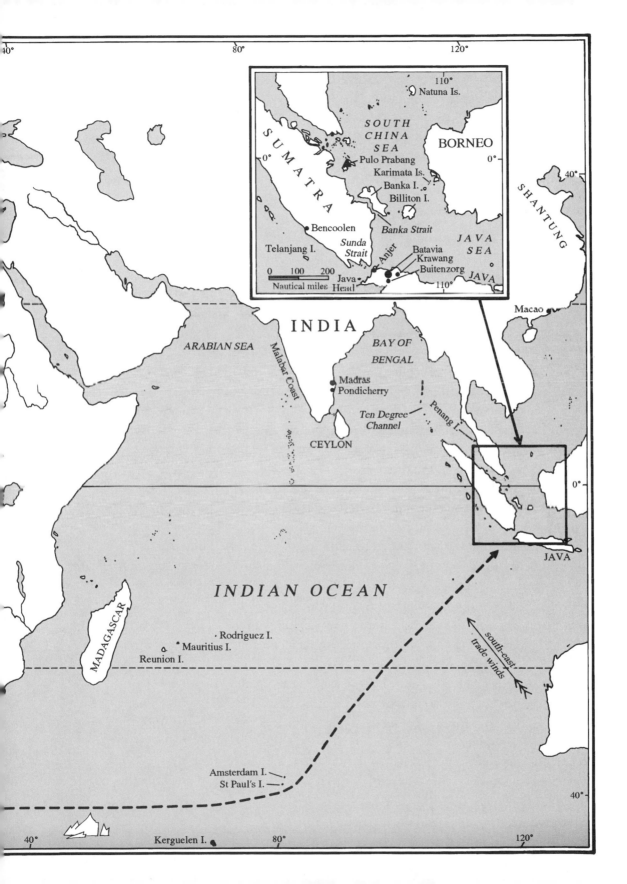

40°   80°   120°

110°
Natuna Is.

SOUTH
CHINA
SEA   BORNEO

0°   0°   40°
Pulo Prabang
Karimata Is.
Banka I.
Billiton I.

Banka Strait

S U M A T R A   SHANTUNG

JAVA
SEA

Bencoolen
Telanjang I.   Sunda
                Strait
        Anjer   Batavia
              Krawang
0 100 200   Buitenzorg   JAVA
Nautical miles Java
              Head   110°

Macao

INDIA

ARABIAN SEA   BAY OF
                              BENGAL

Madras
Pondicherry

Malabar Coast

Ten Degree
Channel   Penang I.

CEYLON

0°

JAVA

INDIAN OCEAN

MADAGASCAR

· Rodriguez I.
Mauritius I.
Reunion I.

south-east
trade winds

Amsterdam I.
St Paul's I.

40°

40°   Kerguelen I.   80°   120°

ought to be (as one would naturally suppose) perfectly well known; notwithstanding which, after having examined the charts of these coasts reputed the best, I venture to say that I have been convinced that there does not exist one with which one can be entirely satisfied" (p. 57).

HERE AND THERE

Batavia

Present-day Jakarta, formerly Batavia, is a seaport city on the northwest coast of Java. The following description of Batavia in 1791 is an edited version from *The Nagle Journal*, the diary of Jacob Nagle, an uneducated American sailor in the British Navy:

> Batavia City is the capital of the island of Java and all the Dutch settlements in the East Indies in general. A great number of the inhabitants are China-men and Malays. The city is handsome—built with white stones. The canals in the principal streets are planted on each side with evergreen trees. The canals have drawbridges that can be lifted every night so that you cannot go out of one street into the other.
>
> Their Indiamen lay outside the bar like a roadstead. There is a strong fort abreast the shipping, but it is at too great a distance to protect them from an enemy. The Dutch are cruel to the Malay slaves. They work them in the heat of the day without mercy, and if they die, heave them overboard like a beast. We had our vessel covered with awnings from stem to stern. Neither did we attempt to work from 8 in the morning till 4 in the afternoon.
>
> Alligators are numerous. A short time before we arrived, a barge's crew of 11 men, going over the bar, was capsized on the flats and devoured, the alligators hauling them off the bottom of the boat, and no other boat dared go to their assistance.
>
> This is the most unhealthy place I ever was in. During the seven weeks we lay here, it was computed, on shore and aboard the Dutch Indiamen, that 4,700 died. When we arrived, we had not a sick man on board, and when we left, we had not a well man on board. The principal ailment was a swelling in the bowels, the other a pain in the breast. The water from the rivers is very bad, being salt peter ground. We had to boil our water in rice or barley, and

then being so hot, it was like physic to us when we had to drink it. . . . We lost several men here and one in Bantom Bay, who had been a messmate of mine for nine years in two ships. I must observe that the captain never prevented any from drinking the liquor while laying here, and those that would not drink any were the first to die, and others who would sit and drink on the forecastle every night were the healthiest men on board.

Corunna or La Coruña

Known to British sailors as "the Groyne" (an etymological perversion of the Spanish name, Coruna), a seaport on the Atlantic Ocean in northwest Spain, famous for its lighthouse thought to have been built by Carthaginians in the first century A.D. In search of the Spanish Armada, Sir Francis Drake burned and sacked the town in 1589. The British Navy defeated the French fleet off Corunna in the Battle of Finisterre in 1747, and in 1805 Admiral Sir Robert Calder captured two ships off Corunna in an action against the French admiral Villeneuve. In 1809 British general Sir John Moore defeated the French forces under Marshal Nicolas-Jean de Dieu Soult at Corunna but was mortally wounded in the battle.

Java

The following description of Java is excerpted from the spring edition of *The Naval Chronicle* for 1812:

> Its direction is nearly east and west: to the south and west, its shores are washed by the southern Indian Ocean; to the northwest lies the island of Sumatra; to the north, Borneo; to the northeast, Celebes; and, to the east, Bali, from which it is separated by a narrow passage, called the Straits of Bali.
>
> The chief produce of the island of Java is pepper, of which the kingdom of Bantam yielded annually to the Dutch East India Company six millions of pounds. . . . The white pepper is only black pepper laid in lime, which occasions the black skin to peel off. Rice is the second produce of Java. In 1767, Java furnished 14,000 tons of rice for Ceylon, Banda, and other settlements. Sugar is also cultivated to a great extent. . . . The next produce of Java is coffee, which was only introduced in the year 1722.
>
> Cotton yarn is an important object of trade in Java. It is spun from the cotton produced in the island, which grows in great abundance. Salt and indigo are native productions of Java. The northeast coast of the island, and part of

the district of Cheribon, furnish a very large quantity of timber, logs, beams, boards, knees, &c., which is not only sufficient for the consumption of Batavia, for ship-building, houses, and domestic uses, but a very considerable quantity of it is annually exported to several of the out factories, and, in particular, to the Cape of Good Hope. (p. 133)

The capture of Java by British forces under the earl of Minto in 1811 marked the end of the Napoleonic War in the East Indies.

Sunda Strait

A channel between the islands of Sumatra and Java, linking the Indian Ocean and the Java Sea. At its narrowest point, the strait is only sixteen miles wide. The volcanic island of Krakatoa lies in the strait. Its eruption in 1883 blew away the northern two-thirds of the island and was the most violent explosion on earth in modern times.

Tristan da Cunha

The largest and northernmost island of a group—also called Tristan da Cunha—of small volcanic islands in the South Atlantic Ocean. The other islands include Gough, Inaccessible, and Nightingale. Tristan was discovered in 1506 by the Portuguese explorer Tristão da Cunha and, because of its remote location, was known for years as Lonely Island.

Despite its isolation, efforts were made to settle the island in the early nineteenth century, as described in the following account from the spring edition of *The Naval Chronicle* for 1813:

Mr. Lambert, the American, who, in 1811, took possession of the island . . . has recently applied to the governor of the Cape of Good Hope, for the patronage and assistance of the British government and East India Company. His agent at the Cape has declared that he would endeavour to afford refreshments to whatever vessels might pass in that track of sea; and that whenever the sanction of the British government should be known, the necessary assistance being given him, he would most solemnly declare himself allied to that government; and, by permission, display the British flag on the island, reserving however always to himself the governorship, provided an equivalent could not be agreed upon. Lord Caledon had granted to his agent a small vessel, to carry from the Cape five industrious families, who had requested leave to emigrate thither, also a few black cattle, sheep, goats, &c. with such other small necessaries as might conduce to the growth and production of the island. (p. 11)

In 1815 the last naval action of the War of 1812 took place off Tristan da Cunha when the British sloop *Penguin* surrendered to the American sloop *Hornet.* The British took formal control of the island in 1816 and sent a party of soldiers to guard against any attempt at rescuing Napoleon, who was exiled on St. Helena.

From the Java Sea
to Sydney Cove

Notwithstanding their inauspicious start, in *The Nutmeg of Consolation*, Aubrey and Maturin continue the voyage they began in book 13, *The Thirteen Gun Salute*. But first they must remove themselves from a rather sticky situation on a deserted island in the Java Sea. Exactly where this island is, O'Brian does not tell us. But the *Diane*'s wreck on an uncharted reef occurs somewhere south of the False Natunas, "two days with a good wind in the proa" (no more than two hundred miles) from Batavia.

Aubrey, Maturin, and the remaining Dianes reach Batavia at last. Here, the benevolent Governor Raffles gives *Gelijkheid*, a 20-gun Dutch ship that has just been raised after having been sunk on purpose to rid it of the "infection," to Aubrey, who rechristens it the *Nutmeg of Consolation*, after one of the epithets of the sultan of Pulo Prabang. In this "tight, sweet, newly-coppered, broad-buttocked little ship," as Aubrey so lyrically describes it, the remaining Dianes now set out with two purposes: most importantly, to rendezvous with the *Surprise* off Kabruang at the east end of the Salibabu Passage, between the Celebes Sea and the Pacific Ocean. As an added incentive for celerity, the Nutmegs hope to catch the *Cornélie*, the 32-gun French frigate that was employed in that country's failed diplomatic effort in Pulo Prabang.

Through his connections, Maturin learns the *Cornélie*'s planned departure date and that she also will be sailing east via the Salibabu Passage, the *Nutmeg*'s intended route. The *Nutmeg* departs from Batavia, laboring east through the Java Sea and north into the Macassar Strait, between Celebes and Borneo.

Too late, Aubrey regrets not having sailed due north to the south end of the Sibutu Passage. He reasons that because of the southwest monsoon, the *Cornélie* would have sailed north above Borneo into the Sulu Sea. Then, to avoid the treacherous Sulu Archipelago, she would have steered south into the Celebes Sea through the narrow Sibutu Passage. This would have been the ideal spot for a close-quarters ambush.

The only solution is to "crack on like smoke and oakum" under towers of sail through the Celebes Sea. En route, the *Surprise* stops the *Alkmaar*, a Dutch merchantman sailing southeast from Manila to Menardo, a Dutch port established in 1657 on the northeast tip of the Celebes. The *Alkmaar* started her water while being chased by pirate proas off the Cagayanes, a group of seven small islands in the north Sulu Sea due south of Manila. She was later stopped by the *Cornélie*, which she is able to report plans to water at Nil Desperandum ("Never Despair"), an island—probably fictional, though there were several islands that went by this name—just west of the Salibabu Passage. At last the *Surprise* and the *Cornélie* convene in a cat-and-mouse duel that carries them into the Salibabu Passage, which lies south of the island of Mindanao in the Philippines.

Following a successful rendezvous with the *Surprise*, the *Nutmeg*—and the *Surprise*'s consorts—the *Triton*, an English letter of marque, and two fat formerly American merchant ships—stand away to the northwest, heading to Batavia via Canton to take advantage of the northeast monsoon. Now with Aubrey and Maturin aboard, the *Surprise* sails east to New South Wales (Australia). It is primarily blue-water sailing, and after a brief stop at the fictional Sweetings Island, where they make an unexpected addition to the crew, Maturin laments to Nathaniel Martin, his surgeon's mate and a fellow naturalist, " 'Nor does he mean to touch at the Solomons, still less to go inside the Great Barrier Reef, or anywhere near it.' " Adds O'Brian, "They both shook their heads sadly."

At last, ensconced in Sydney Cove, Maturin and Martin make up for lost naturalizing opportunities. They explore the coastal wilds north of Sydney, travel inland toward the Blue Mountains—where they happily dine on grilled wombat—and visit the forests of the Hunter River. Maturin even has the thrilling experience of handling a male *Ornithorhynchus*, also known as the water mole or platypus.

NEXT PAGE: On the recently recovered *Nutmeg*, Aubrey sets off with two goals in mind. Most important is his rendezvous with Thomas Pullings and the *Surprise* near Kabruang Island, south of Mindanao. His other objective is to capture the *Cornélie*, the ship belonging to the French mission at Pulo Prabang.

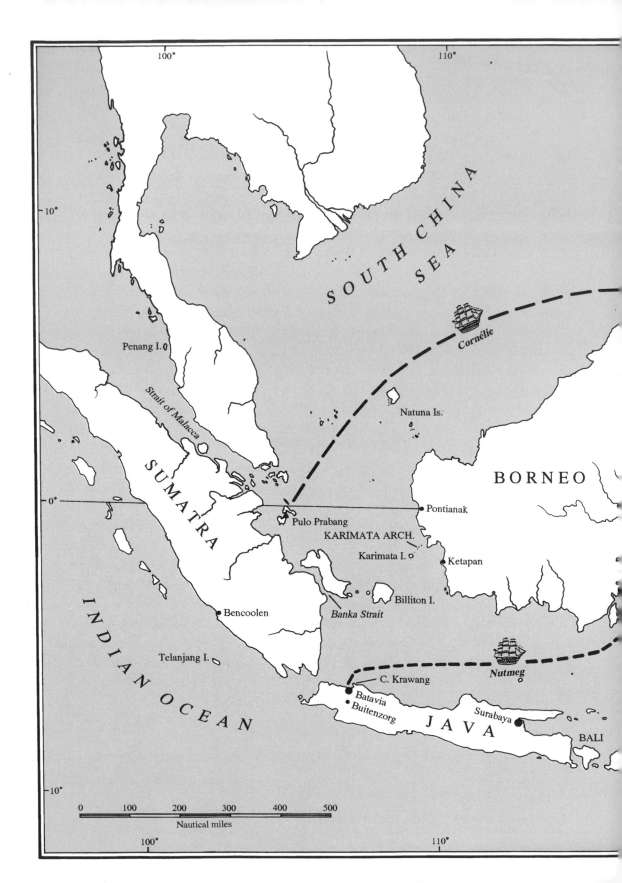

100°

110°

10°

SOUTH CHINA

SEA

Cornélie

Penang I.

Natuna Is.

Strait of Malacca

BORNEO

0°

SUMATRA

Pulo Prabang

Pontianak

KARIMATA ARCH.

Karimata I.

Ketapan

Billiton I.

Banka Strait

Bencoolen

INDIAN

Telanjang I.

Nutmeg

C. Krawang

Batavia

OCEAN

Buitenzorg

JAVA

Surabaya

BALI

10°

0   100   200   300   400   500

Nautical miles

100°

110°

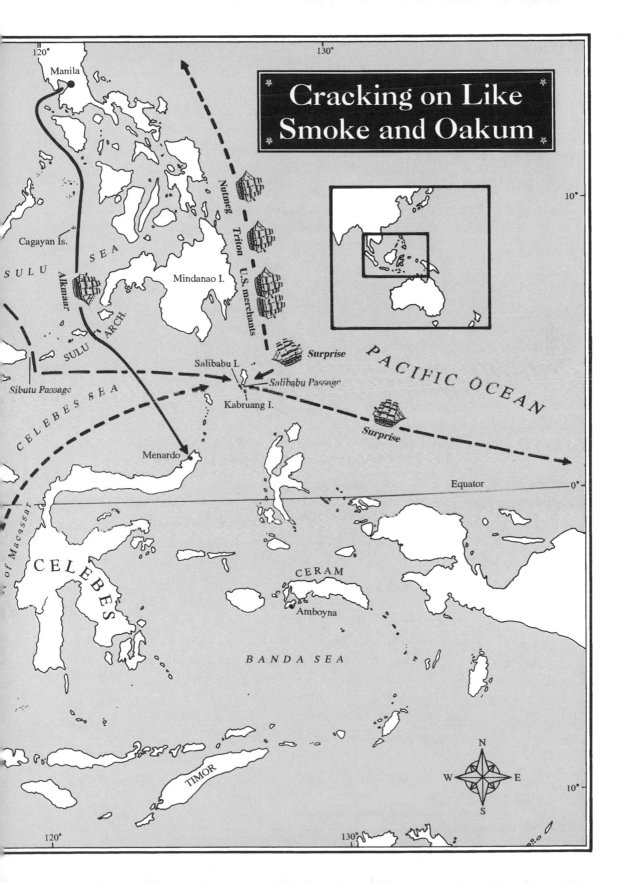

Cracking on Like Smoke and Oakum

Manila

120°

130°

10°

Cagayan Is.

SULU SEA

Alkmaar

SULU ARCH.

Sibutu Passage

CELEBES SEA

Nutmeg

Triton

U.S. merchants

Mindanao I.

Salibabu I.

Salibabu Passage

Kabruang I.

Menardo

of Macassar

CELEBES

Surprise

PACIFIC OCEAN

Surprise

Equator

0°

CERAM

Amboyna

BANDA SEA

TIMOR

N

W   E

S

120°

130°

10°

A scene involving the *Waaksamkeyd* at an island south of Mindanao. This engraving is from an original drawing by Governor Hunter and represents a quarrel that took place between the natives of an island off the south point of Mindanao and the crew of the *Waaksamkeyd* transport, on board of which were embarked the officers and company of His Majesty's late ship *Sirius*. The vessel wore Dutch colors, because the natives were known to be in the interest of the Dutch, as can be seen by the fact that the Rajah's boat wears the flag of that nation. (Fall 1801 edition of *The Naval Chronicle*, p. 381.)

HERE AND THERE

Antipodes

A term used in Britain to refer to Australia and New Zealand. They are so called because they lie at the opposite end of the earth (or antipodes) from England. The word comes from the Greek *antipous*, meaning "with the feet opposite." Also, specifically, the Antipodes Islands, a group of uninhabited rocky islands in the South Pacific Ocean, 350 miles off the southeastern coast of New Zealand.

Java Sea

A shallow section of the Pacific Ocean between Java and Borneo. The following cruising instructions for the Java Sea were issued by the commanding officer on the Eastern station in the years 1807 to 1808. They were published in the spring edition of *The Naval Chronicle* for 1813:

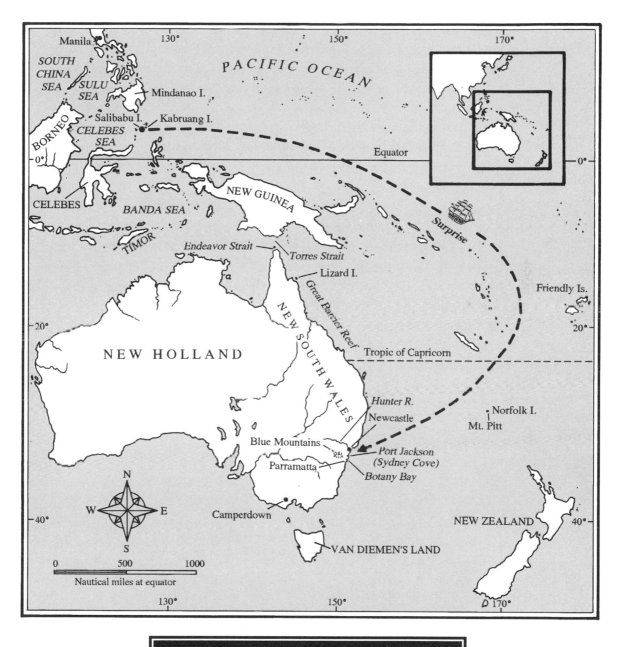

✳ A Blue-Water Sail to Sydney Cove ✳

Her true captain returned to the quarterdeck, the *Surprise* sails east to New South Wales with nary a stop for the naturalists to indulge their curiosity.

The following circumstances must be particularly attended to by ships going down the Strait of Malacca and into the Javan Seas. On leaving Malacca, care should be taken to circulate a report that you are going quite contrary to the route you intend, for, from particular advantages attending the navigation of small craft, such information will precede you underhand through all the Strait, and to the eastward.

In falling in with prows, care should be observed in searching them as very often great property is concealed in places where no European would suspect, and it has been discovered that the Dutch have carried on correspondences in the hollow of large bamboos, thrown carelessly into small prows. . . . On no account let any of your smaller boats board any prow that is out of gun-shot from the ship. But be particular in sending your largest boats well manned and armed, and in directing them never to approach such prow or vessel end-on, as they are often defended by two heavy guns placed either forward or aft. The most contemptible-looking craft fallen in with in these seas must be searched in the most minute manner both for property and papers.

A view of Canton River, China. (Fall 1811 edition of *The Naval Chronicle*, p. 148.)

After you get off Carimatta, great caution should be used in proceeding eastward as the currents are so uncertain and variable, and the dangers so numerous, that no dependence is to be placed on anything but constant good look-out, night and day.

In the State of Allas, on the Lombok side at the village of Laboagee (its Malay name), stock, bullocks, and goats may be gotten in great abundance; and on the island of Timor, at the port of Diely, buffalos and hogs. At Diely, in particular, permit no water to be taken on board, nor your boats' crews to use any thereof while on duty ashore. If you should go through the Strait of Macassar, at Pasir on the Borneo side, and to the northward of that at Goatty, a little stock may be procured. (p. 314)

New South Wales

Now a state on the east coast of Australia, New South Wales was discovered in 1770 by the British explorer Captain James Cook, who claimed it for Great Britain. Cook,

A view of the Coupang River on the island of Timor. Now in the possession of the Dutch, the island produces primarily sandal wood, wax, and honey. There are many Chinese on Timor, who carry on a considerable traffic with China in these articles and particularly in birds' nests, out of which the Chinese make a soup considered by them to be the greatest of delicacies. (Fall 1806 edition of *The Naval Chronicle*, p. 129.)

commanding the *Endeavour*, was financed and accompanied by the wealthy botanist Joseph Banks. The expedition first landed on the shores of Botany Bay, which Cook initially named "Stingray Bay" and then renamed in honor of Banks's activities there. Eighteen years later, Captain Arthur Phillip landed at Botany Bay with orders from the British government to establish a penal colony there, but Phillip moved the settlement a few miles north to Port Jackson, which he deemed a more suitable site.

Port Jackson

An inlet on the southeastern coast of Australia at the mouth of the Parramatta River, Port Jackson is one of the world's finest natural harbors. In Charles Nordhoff and James Norman Hall's fact-based novel *Botany Bay* (1941), the fictional character Hugh Tallant, a convicted felon who has been sent in the First Fleet under Captain Phillip to form the penal colony on New South Wales, describes their arrival in Port Jackson in the year 1788: "Sailing in past the southern head, with sheets slacked off we opened the vast, landlocked harbour which stretched away for miles to the south and west. The wind was cut off by the high land as we turned southward, and we furled our sails. All gazed at the still waters opening before us in hushed wonder and delight, scarcely venturing to speak in this enchanted place. The great Harbour, sheltered from every storm and ruffled only by light cat's-paws off the land, extended before us, branching in coves and bays separated by wooded points, as far as the eye could reach. . . . Forests of gum and cedar stood at the head of almost every cove. Clouds of snow-white cockatoos, their plumage gleaming in the sunlight, passed from one wooded promontory to the next; bright-coloured parakeets rose in thousands from the trees, with harsh chatterings, as if in protest at this violation of their sanctuary. . . . We were the first white men to gaze on these scenes of unsullied primaeval loveliness, and I shall recollect them to my last day" (p. 130).

Named (for Deputy Admiralty Secretary George Jackson), but not explored, by Cook, the port is known today as Sydney Harbour. The city of Sydney sits on its southern shore.

Sulu Archipelago

A 180-mile chain of more than nine hundred islands and numerous coral reefs that extends from Basilan Island in the Philippines to northeast Borneo and separates the Sulu Sea from the Celebes Sea. The islands were ruled by the Moro sultans, who were given to piracy.

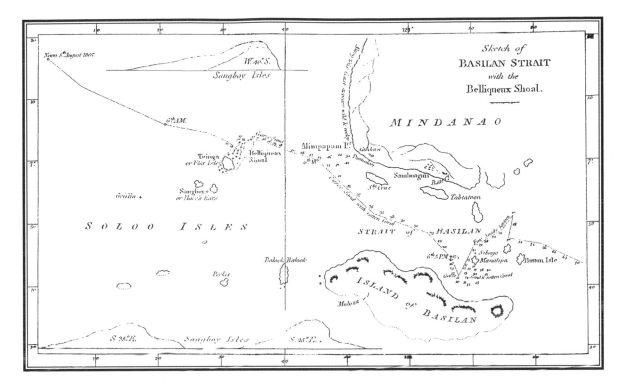

A chart of the Basilan Strait. A ship intending to water at Maloza may anchor near the island. The village of Maloza is about a mile up the river, the narrow entrance of which is not discernible till close to it. Although the river has been recommended as a good watering place, it is so only for vessels which are well armed; and it is so narrow for some distance below the village, that there is not room to row the oars. If a ship be obliged to water here, two armed boats ought to be sent together; and when the water is found to be fresh, it is not advisable to proceed higher up to the village on account of the perfidy of the natives.

One may do well to heed the warning implicit in Horsburgh's "Directions": "In March, 1793, the *Anna*'s longboat made three trips to this river for water: the inhabitants seemed very friendly, and the fisherman, who acted as guide, endeavoured to persuade us to land, saying that we would be well treated at the village, that there were only women and children in it, the men being out fishing. This apparently seemed the case, for few men were seen, but plenty of women came to the boat with poultry and more to barter with the crew for handkerchiefs, knives, and trinkets. I, however, discovered from one of the boat's crew, who understood the language that there were more than 100 armed men concealed behind the bushes, and he overheard two persons appoint the time of an attack. But fortunately their design was frustrated, for like true assassins, they had not the courage to make the attack, because three Europeans in the boat kept arms constantly in their hands." (Fall 1813 edition of *The Naval Chronicle*, p. 215.)

Sydney Cove

Founded as a penal settlement by Captain Arthur Phillip in 1788, Sydney Cove, in Port Jackson, was the first seat of British authority in Australia. Phillip named the settlement for Viscount Sydney, the British home secretary. Today it lies at the heart of the modern city of Sydney and is often called Circular Quay.

An Urgent Detour to the Not-So-Pacific Island of Moahu

In book 15, *The Truelove*, Aubrey and Maturin continue the eastward voyage that they began in book 13, *The Thirteen Gun Salute*. Having accomplished their diplomatic mission in the Malay Archipelago, rendezvoused with the *Surprise* near the island of Mindanao, and resupplied at Sydney in New South Wales, they now plan to sail in the *Surprise* across the South Pacific Ocean via Norfolk Island and Easter Island to the west coast of South America. Here, Maturin will seek to perform yet another diplomatic service for the king in Peru and Chile.

But once again the *Surprise* becomes sidetracked on urgent official business. This time new instructions arrive via the cutter *Eclair* near Norfolk Island—some 870 sea miles from Sydney, but not far enough to prevent express delivery of official orders. Told to resolve a power struggle on the fictional British island of Moahu in favor of whichever side he perceives is most likely to acknowledge the king's sovereignty, Aubrey alters course, sailing directly for the Fiji Islands. Contrary winds, however, cause the *Surprise* to veer east toward Tonga, or the Friendly Islands, an archipelago of about 150 volcanic and coral islands.

Here the Surprises touch at Annamooka for fresh supplies and water and gain some valuable information from the master of the whaler *Daisy* about the volatile state of affairs on Moahu and the plight of the British merchant ship *Truelove*.

O'Brian informs us at various times that the volcanic island of Moahu is "to the south of the Sandwich group" and "no great way from Hawaii." In fact, the name

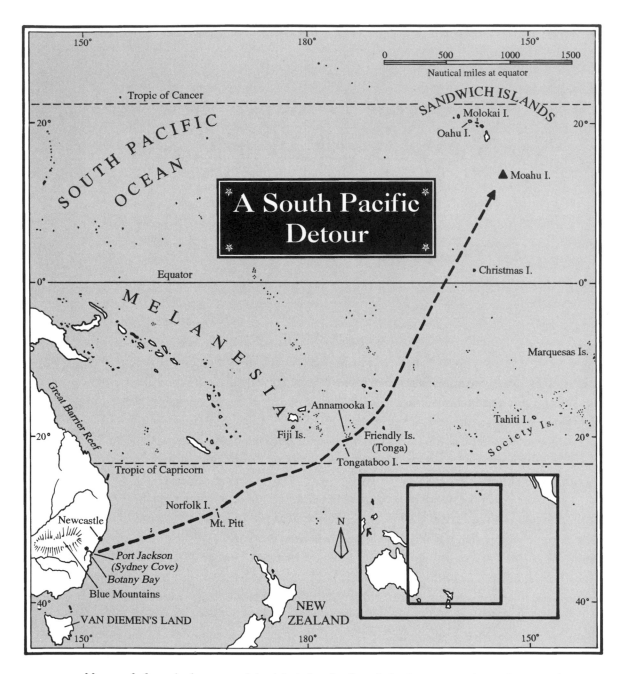

Never safe from the long arm of the Admiralty, the *Surprise* is given yet another task to complete before she carries Maturin to South America. A cutter catches up with her off Norfolk Island to deliver the orders, and she detours through the Friendly Islands to Moahu.

"Moahu" seems to be inspired by a phonetic combination of "Woahoo" and "Mowee," early renditions of "Oahu" and "Maui," respectively. We also know that Moahu belongs to the British, "Captain Cook having taken possession of the archipelago in 1779," the same year Cook was murdered at Kealakua Bay, Hawaii. The *Surprise* approaches Christmas Island, which was discovered by Cook in 1777, from the south. At about a three days' sail from Moahu it appears on the eastern horizon to starboard. Moahu—where the novel's action reaches its climax—would lie then at about 10°N, somewhere between the Line Islands and the Sandwich (Hawaiian) Islands.

HERE AND THERE

Annamooka Island
One of the Friendly Islands, an archipelago (also called Tonga) of more than 150 islands in the southwest Pacific Ocean about four hundred miles east of Fiji. Captain James Cook visited Annamooka in 1773 and again in 1777. William Bligh, captain of the *Bounty*, stopped here in 1789, and in Sir John Barrow's *Mutiny of the Bounty*, Bligh reports, " 'I walked to the west part of the bay, where some plants and seeds had been sown by Captain Cook; and had the satisfaction to see, in a plantation close by, about twenty fine pineapple plants . . .' " (p. 48).

Christmas Island
Known today as Kiritimati, Christmas Island is one of the Line Islands, in the central Pacific Ocean south of Hawaii. At 230 square miles, Christmas Island is the Pacific's largest coral atoll. It was discovered by Captain Cook on Christmas Eve, 1777.

Easter Island
A volcanic island in the Pacific Ocean, about twenty-three hundred miles west of Chile, famous for its monolithic stone figures thought to have been carved by the island's original Polynesian population in the early centuries A.D. The island is so named because Jacob Roggeveen, a Dutch captain, discovered it on Easter Sunday in 1722. Captain Cook landed there in 1774.

Nootka Sound
An inlet of the Pacific Ocean on Vancouver Island, in the southwest corner of Canada. Captain Cook spent a month at Nootka Sound in 1778, and the British explorer John

Meares erected a trading post there, near more than twenty Indian villages. The Spanish claimed the region in 1789, and the resulting controversy almost led to war between Britain and Spain. The issue was settled in Britain's favor by the Nootka Sound Convention in 1790.

Norfolk Island

A thirteen-square-mile volcanic island in the South Pacific about 930 miles northeast of Sydney. Norfolk Island was discovered by Captain Cook in 1774 and operated as a British penal colony from 1788 to 1813. In 1856 the descendants of the *Bounty* mutineers would move here from Pitcairn Island.

The following description of Norfolk Island is adapted from *The Nagle Journal*, the diary of Jacob Nagle, an American sailor aboard HMS *Sirius*, who grounded at Norfolk Island in 1790:

> Some books say there is good anchorage at Norfolk Island, but they are mistaken. It is iron-bound all around, with coral rock and heavy surf, and all ships while I remained on the island had to lie to or off and on while discharging or taking in.
>
> When we first landed, the gannets—a sea fowl as big as a goose—would come open-mouthed to you, but we destroyed a good many and they left the island. The principal sea birds on the island were mount pitters and mutton birds. The mount pitters were about the size of a pigeon but fuller in the body, with a hawk bill and web foot. They bred in the valleys of Mount Pit. The mutton birds were rather smaller than the mount pitters. These birds, as God would have it, were the saving of us as they were the chief living we had while they lasted, beside the wild mountain cabbage tree that grew on the island.
>
> There were but few land birds on the island excepting quail, a few parrots, parakeets that fed on the wild red pepper, and some wild pigeons of the same color as our tame pigeons, but we reduced them a great deal before we left. We never found any kind of wild beast, snakes or toads, or anything that was venomous during the time we were on the island.
>
> The wood that grows on the island is in general pine, and it grows up to an amazing height and thickness. We were a considerable time employed in cutting down trees and sawing them for masts and spars for shipping. But we found they were not serviceable as it was white pine, brittle and worm-eaten, but useful for building houses.

We had two cobles built by our carpenters to go out fishing when the weather would permit. The groupers were plentiful at the west end of the island, but the misfortune was that we could not go out through the surf unless it was a very calm day and without wind. Sometimes it would be five or six weeks that we could not go out, and when we did, the moment a breeze sprang up on that side of the island, the flag would be hoisted, which meant to come in immediately, or otherwise the surf would rise so quick and high that it would be impossible to come in and then we would have to go around the island on the lee side, which would be very dangerous. (pp. 117–131)

Tahiti

Also known as Otaheite or King George's Island, Tahiti is the largest of the Windward group of the Society Islands, which are situated in the central South Pacific. Part of French Polynesia, the Society Islands were discovered by the Portuguese navigator Pedro Fernandes de Queirós in 1607. In 1767 British Navy Captain Samuel Wallis claimed Tahiti for Britain, but the French navigator Louis-Antoine de Bougainville made the same claim for France in 1768. Captain Cook visited Tahiti in 1769, 1773, and 1777.

In 1788 Captain Bligh's *Bounty* landed in Tahiti, and in Nordhoff and Hall's fictional but fact-based *Mutiny on the Bounty*, Midshipman Roger Byam describes his first view of the island:

Since that morning so many years ago, I have sailed all the seas of the world and visited most of the islands in them, including the West Indies, and the Asiatic Archipelago. But of all the islands I have seen, none approaches Tahiti in loveliness. . . .

We were skirting the windward coast of Taiarapu, the richest and loveliest part of the island, and I could not take my eyes off the land. In the foreground, a mile or more off-shore, a reef of coral broke the roll of the sea, and the calm waters of the lagoon inside formed a highway on which the Indians travel back and forth in their canoes. Behind the inner beach was the narrow belt of flat land where the rustic dwellings of the people were scattered picturesquely among their neat plantations of the *ava* and the cloth plant, shaded by groves of breadfruit and coconut. In the background were the mountains—rising fantastically in turrets, spires, and precipices, wooded to their very tops. Innumerable waterfalls plunged over the cliffs and hung like

A view of Oparray Harbor on Island of Otaheite [Tahiti]. The native canoes sometimes carry a very lofty narrow sail of matting. In very smooth water they are able to ply to windward, but the natives never attempt to go any distance with an adverse wind; so that from Orieteea [Raiatea], Huhahayney [Huahine], and the other Society Islands, a voyage to Otaheite is never undertaken but with a westerly wind, and the same from Otaheite to Maiteea [Mehitea]. (Fall 1811 edition of *The Naval Chronicle*, p. 141.)

suspended threads of silver, many of them a thousand feet or more in height and visible at a great distance against the background of dark green. Seen for the first time by European eyes, this coast is like nothing else on our workaday planet; a landscape, rather, of some fantastic dream. (pp. 65–66)

South America at Last

Having resolved matters in Moahu in favor of the natives to the south, the *Surprise* now sets off in hot pursuit of the 22-gun American privateer *Franklin*. Sailing on a bowline, the two ships use the northeast trade winds to carry them as fast as possible in a southeasterly direction toward the equator and Peru. They trade shots from their bow- and stern-chasers, each praying for that lucky strike to disable the other just long enough to end the affair. Growing more desperate, the *Franklin* starts its water and sends some of its guns into the deep. It is not the ships' thundering broadsides that bring this action to its climax, however, but one of an altogether different nature.

As the two ships, having resolved their differences, proceed toward Callao, Peru, the port near Lima, they encounter an American whaler. From one of her crew, Aubrey learns that the *Alastor*, a four-masted French pirate ship, is lying in wait in the Chinchas—a group of small islands off the coast of central Peru—for an English ship about to sail from Callao. Aubrey decides to pursue the *Alastor*.

At long last, Maturin is set down in Peru to begin his covert effort to dislodge the Spanish and undermine French efforts to gain influence. But the affair is not as simple as he might have wished. Before he can bring his plan to fruition, his cover is blown. Maturin is forced to take to the high Andes in order to escape from Peru. Fortunately, he has as his companion and guide an Incan named Eduardo, a native of the high mountains, who has climbed Pichincha, a 15,173-foot volcano northwest of Quito, as well as the 20,561-foot Chimborazo and the 19,347-foot Cotopaxi, both in what is today north-central Ecuador.

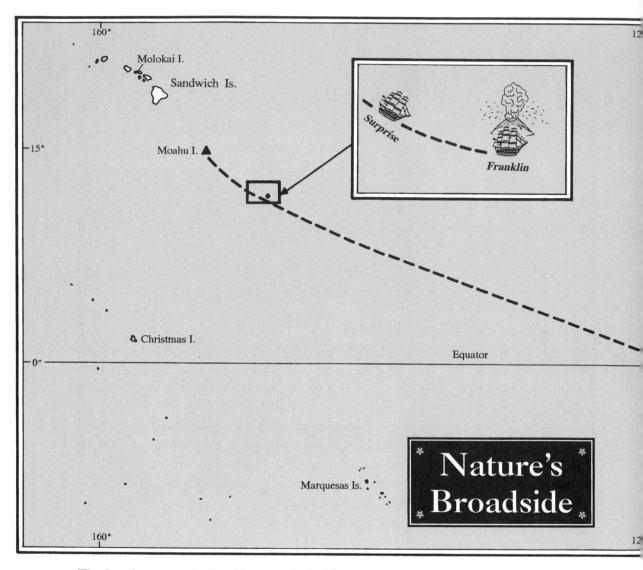

The *Surprise* pursues the *Franklin* across the Pacific toward South America when a timely volcanic eruption interrupts the chase.

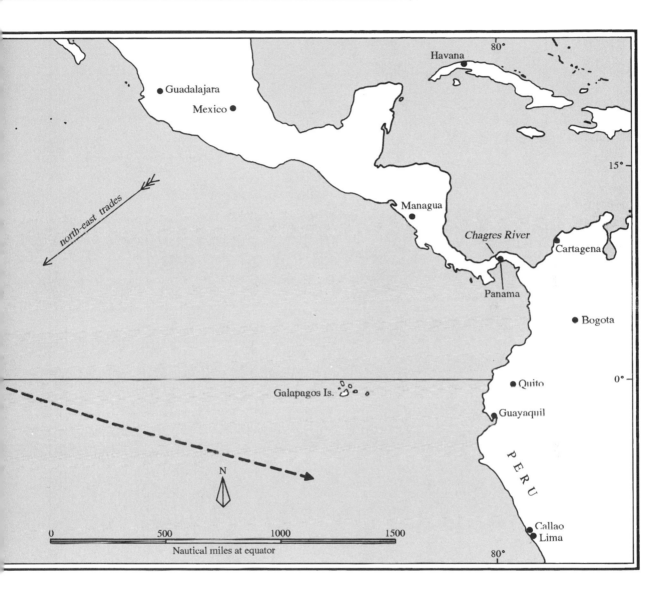

Havana

80°

Guadalajara

Mexico

15°

north-east trades

Managua

Chagres River

Cartagena

Panama

Bogota

0°

Quito

Galapagos Is.

Guayaquil

N

P E R U

500   1000   1500
Nautical miles at equator

Callao
Lima

80°

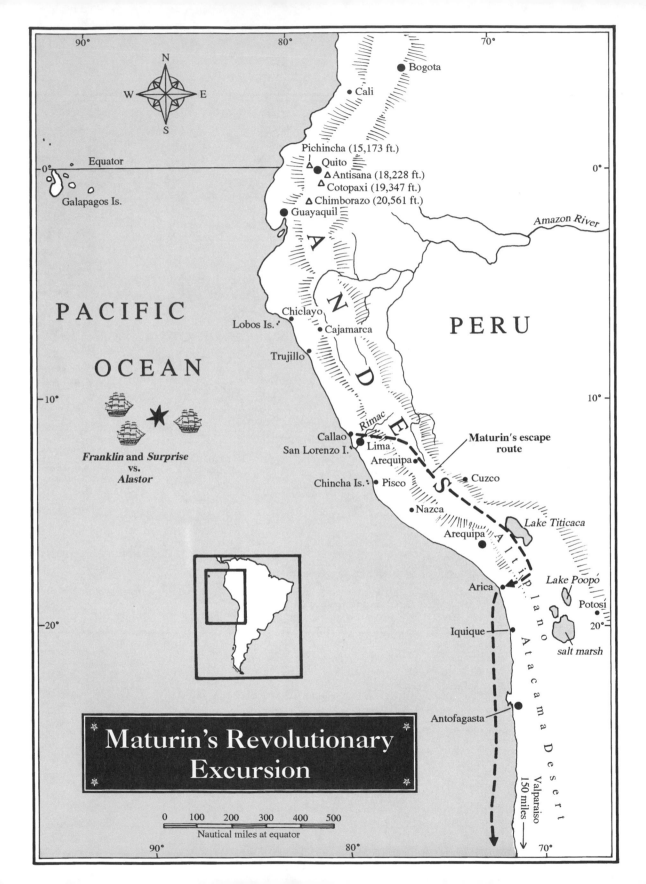

Maturin's Revolutionary Excursion

N
W   E
S

90°   80°   70°

Bogota

Cali

Equator   0°

Galapagos Is.

Pichincha (15,173 ft.)
Quito
Antisana (18,228 ft.)
Cotopaxi (19,347 ft.)
Chimborazo (20,561 ft.)
Guayaquil

Amazon River

PACIFIC

OCEAN

PERU

Chiclayo
Lobos Is.
Cajamarca

Trujillo

Franklin and *Surprise*
vs.
Alastor

Callao
San Lorenzo I.
Lima
Arequipa

Chincha Is.
Pisco

Nazca

Maturin's escape route

Cuzco

Lake Titicaca

Arequipa

Lake Poopó

Arica

Potosi

Iquique

salt marsh

Antofagasta

Atacama Desert

Valparaiso
150 miles

0 100 200 300 400 500
Nautical miles at equator

90°   80°   70°

Traveling south through the mountains, over the Altiplano, or high puna—the cold, arid plateau between the two great chains of the Cordilleras at an elevation of more than 10,500 feet—to Lake Titicaca, and then via coasting vessel, he drives on to convene with Aubrey and the *Surprise* in Valparaiso, Chile, in some two months' time.

Despite the political failure, Maturin's excursion to Peru is not entirely in vain. In addition to taking advantage of some prime naturalizing opportunities (with yet another brush with death in the process), he gains information that just might both further the king's goals and make the crew of the *Surprise* very much the richer. Three American China ships, it seems, will be passing through the Straits le Maire in a westerly direction at approximately the same time that the *Surprise* will be rounding Cape Horn in an easterly direction. Arriving in Valparaiso, Maturin learns from his Argentine connections that the Canton-bound Boston merchantmen left Buenos Aires on Candlemas Day (the February 2 celebration of the purification of the Virgin Mary and the presentation of Christ in the Temple). Aubrey decides to lie in wait for the American ships off the treacherous point of Cape Horn, near the Diego Ramirez Islands. Unfortunately, the weather is worse than expected, and so is the company.

When the rudder of the *Surprise* breaks, Aubrey tells Maturin that he intends to "bear away for the Cape" if he can't "haul up for St. Helena." He is referring, in the former case, to the Cape of Good Hope at the southern tip of Africa and, in the latter, to the South Atlantic British island to which Napoleon will later be exiled. Fortunately, well before they "raise the Table Mountain" (a thirty-five-hundred-foot peak at the northern end of the Cape Peninsula), another solution to their troubles presents itself.

HERE AND THERE

Callao

The chief seaport of Peru, situated eight miles west of Lima on Callao Bay, a fine natural harbor protected by an offshore island and a narrow peninsula. Founded in 1537 by Francisco Pizarro, Callao was frequently attacked by English and Dutch pirates. A tidal wave and earthquake demolished the city in 1746. Its fortress, built in the eighteenth century, was the last stronghold of Spanish Royalist forces in South America; they capitulated in 1826.

When political matters take a turn for the worse, Maturin heads for the mountains. His rapid trek to the south does not preclude some opportunities for naturalizing in the high Andes.

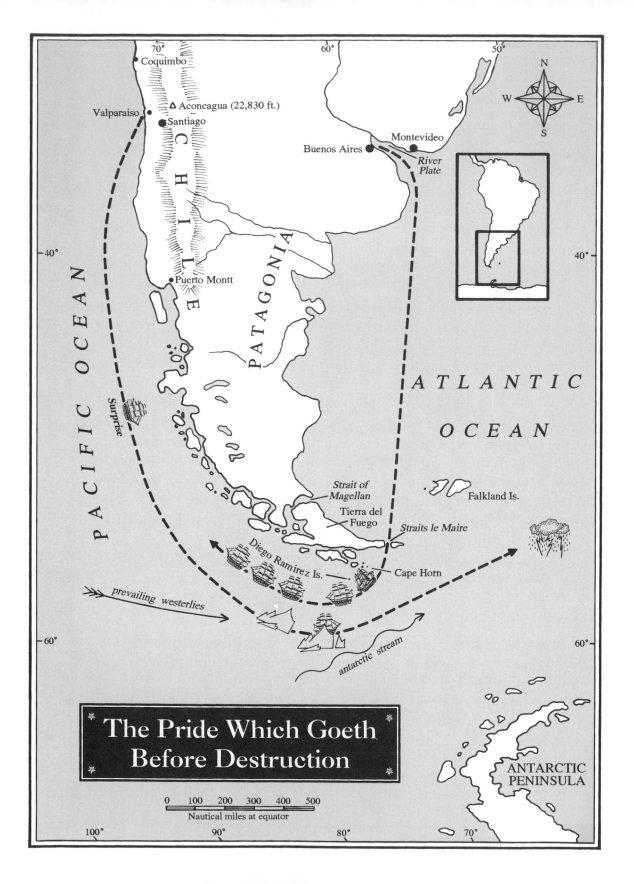

70°   60°   50°

Coquimbo

△ Aconcagua (22,830 ft.)

Valparaiso

Santiago

C
H
I
L
E

Montevideo

Buenos Aires

River
Plate

N
W   E
S

40°   40°

Puerto Montt

P
A
T
A
G
O
N
I
A

PACIFIC OCEAN

Surprise

ATLANTIC

OCEAN

Strait of
Magellan

Tierra del
Fuego

Falkland Is.

Straits le Maire

Diego Ramirez Is.

Cape Horn

prevailing westerlies

60°   60°

antarctic stream

ANTARCTIC
PENINSULA

The Pride Which Goeth
Before Destruction

0   100   200   300   400   500

Nautical miles at equator

100°   90°   80°   70°

Chile

A ribbon of land stretching more than twenty-six hundred miles from Peru to the southern tip of South America at Cape Horn, including the larger part of the Tierra del Fuego Archipelago. O'Brian's novel *The Unknown Shore* is based on the story of the shipwreck of the *Wager*, one of the ships that rounded the Horn with Commodore Anson in 1740, and the subsequent desperate journey of part of her crew along the wild southern coast of Chile to the town of Chiloé.

Nowhere is Chile more than 221 miles wide, and it has an average width of only 110 miles. The Andes Mountains, reaching to more than twenty-two thousand feet above sea level, separate the country from Argentina and Bolivia. The first European exploration of Chile was made in 1536 by Diego de Almagro, a Spanish explorer who made the voyage to the New World with Pizarro. The European settlers who followed encountered fierce resistance from the native Araucanian Indians and met with a number of natural disasters.

In 1810 the Creoles (Chilean-born Spaniards) revolted against the Spanish Crown, but independence was not achieved until 1817 at the Battle of Chacabuco, where the Spanish forces were decisively defeated by Chileans and Argentines led by Bernardo O'Higgins and José de San Martín. O'Higgins was elected supreme director, but by 1830 he was in exile, and conservative landowners and merchants controlled a centralized government.

Cuzco

Known as the "City of the Sun," Cuzco, which sits in a broad valley of the Andes eleven thousand feet above sea level, was the capital of the vast Inca empire. According to legend, it was founded in the eleventh century by Manco Capac, the first Inca ruler. Cuzco is famed for its Temple of the Sun, the fortress of Sacsahuaman, and other buildings made of enormous stone blocks cut so precisely that they need no mortar. The city's temples and palaces were decorated with an abundance of gold and silver from all parts of the Inca empire.

In 1533 Pizarro destroyed the city and plundered its treasures. His followers built a new city on the site, often incorporating the ruins of the Incan buildings and adorning their churches with the looted wealth. Under Spanish rule, Cuzco flourished as an art center, and a university was founded in 1672.

As a parting present, Maturin is informed of several American merchantmen rounding Cape Horn. But he is not told that an escort has joined them.

188 Harbors and High Seas

Diego Ramirez

Located sixty miles southwest of Cape Horn, Diego Ramirez is the southernmost group of islands in the Tierra del Fuego Archipelago at the southern tip of South America.

Hull

Also known as Kingston upon Hull, a seaport in northeastern England on the River Hull where it joins the Humber River estuary. Founded in 1219 and granted a royal charter in 1227, the city grew slowly until the late eighteenth century, when England's trade with northern continental Europe increased and the port of Hull developed rapidly.

Potosi

At 13,800 feet, Potosi, in what is today southwest Bolivia, ranks as one of the highest cities in the world. Spaniards founded the town in 1545 after silver was discovered in the area. Its population peaked in 1650 at about 160,000 people, but by 1825 this number had dropped to around 8,000.

Great Guns on the Coasts of Africa and Ireland

At long last, Aubrey and Maturin return to England after a protracted and arduous circumnavigation that began in book 13, *The Thirteen Gun Salute*. When *The Commodore* opens, the *Surprise* and HMS *Berenice* are in the chops of the Channel, somewhere between Ushant, France, on the starboard bow and the Scillies, a group of 140 tiny islands off the tip of southwest England, on the larboard. They soon part, the *Surprise* steering toward her home port, Shelmerston, in the West Country, and the *Berenice* heading for Portsmouth—or, as sailors liked to call it, "Pompey"—which, although it was frequently considered a western port by authorities, was at least central if not east.

When Maturin reaches Barham Down and finds that Diana's horses have been sent to Doncaster, in South Yorkshire, and that she last wrote from Harrogate, in North Yorkshire, he has to make new arrangements for his daughter, Brigid. He also finds it necessary to make a personal voyage first from Portsmouth to London to pick up his fortune and then back to Shelmerston before proceeding to Spain, where he can leave his makeshift family in safe hands. O'Brian describes the trip, beginning in front of Southsea Castle in Portsmouth harbor, in some detail, and many of the place names can be found on the map "Maturin's Private Voyage to London," on the following page.

NEXT PAGE: " 'There is no such thing as obligation between you and me, brother,' said Jack," lending Maturin the clipper *Ringle* along with Reade, Bonden, and a pair of Shelmerston's finest smugglers for a speedy voyage to London.

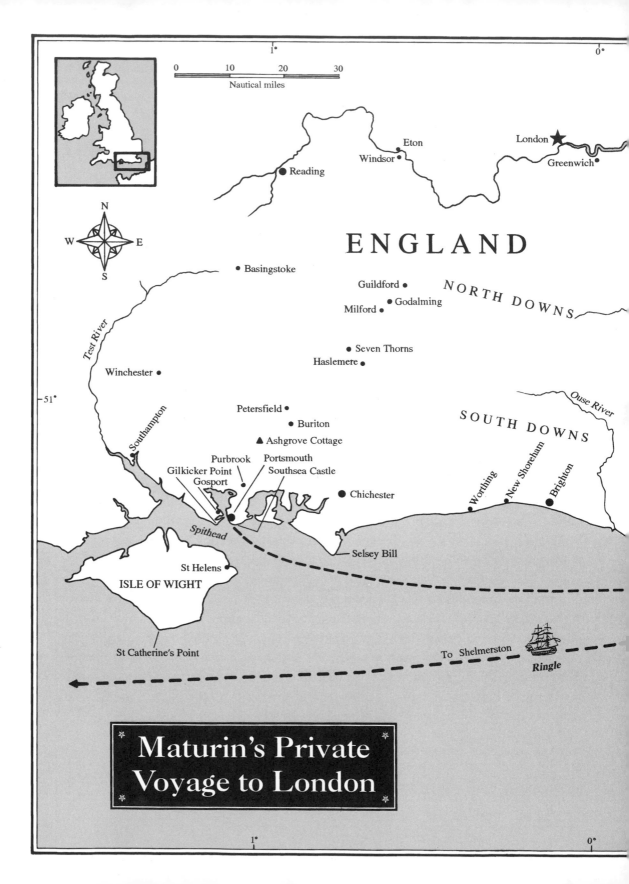

Maturin's Private Voyage to London

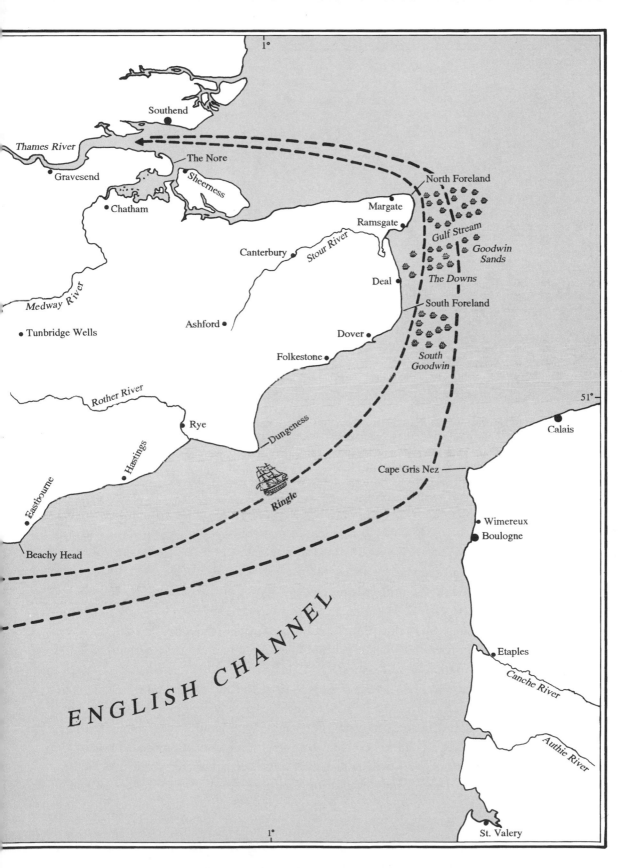

Southend

Thames River

Gravesend

The Nore

Sheerness

Chatham

North Foreland

Margate

Ramsgate

Gulf Stream

Goodwin Sands

Canterbury

Stour River

The Downs

Deal

South Foreland

Medway River

Ashford

Dover

Tunbridge Wells

Folkestone

South Goodwin

Rother River

Dungeness

Rye

Ringle

Calais

Hastings

Cape Gris Nez

Eastbourne

Wimereux

Boulogne

Beachy Head

51°

Etaples

Canche River

ENGLISH CHANNEL

Authie River

St. Valery

1°

1°

A view of Southsea Castle. Southsea Castle is situated nearly at the entrance of Portsmouth harbor. This view of the castle as it appears from Spithead is engraved from an original by Pocock. In the foreground is a Swedish galliot on a wind standing out from Portsmouth. (Fall 1806 edition of *The Naval Chronicle*, p. 232.)

On their trip up the Thames, when the sky clears and shows "Greenwich in all its splendour," Mould, the Shelmerston smuggler, complains about the money sailors pour into Greenwich. He is referring to the "seaman's sixpence," a deduction from the monthly wage of all seamen used to support Greenwich Royal Hospital in its care of wounded, disabled, and elderly seamen as well as to provide for sailors' widows and orphans. When they arrive, Maturin catches a wherry to the Temple Stairs, steps leading from the Thames up to the Temple. Later he is accompanied by Parson Hinksey as far as the Temple Bar, which is not a drinking establishment but the gate marking the formal entrance to the City of London.

On the voyage south, Maturin reveals to Padeen Colman that he is to watch over Clarissa Oaks and Brigid in Avila, an eleventh-century walled city about fifty miles northwest of Madrid, where they will be lodging temporarily in a convent. Before touching at Corunna, in Galicia (a region and ancient kingdom of northwest Spain), the *Ringle*, in evasive maneuvers, weathers nearby Cape Vares, literally within a biscuit toss (see the map "An Unexpected Round-trip," on page 151). Lighter some six tons of treasure and three passengers, who will travel overland to Avila, the *Ringle* joins Aubrey, on board the *Bellona*, and the rest of his squadron—the *Stately*, the *Aurora*, and the *Thames*, along with the 22-gun *Laurel* and the 20-gun *Camilla* and several small brigs and cutters—off the coast of Portugal.

At the 31st parallel, Aubrey opens his orders and finds out—to his utmost satisfaction—that his mission is really twofold. First he is to harass the slavers on the west coast of Africa—a feint. His second, secret mission is to double back and engage a French squadron that will be departing from Brest with the goal to "liberate" Ireland. To preserve time and to be effective, the strike in Africa must be fast and furious.

Off Freetown, Sierra Leone, Aubrey's squadron, with the assistance of James Wood, a former shipmate of Aubrey's and now the governor of Sierra Leone, ostentatiously destroys the *Nancy*, a slaver captured two weeks out of Whydah, one of the slave-trading centers of northwestern Africa. The squadron works south and east along the Grain, Ivory, and Gold coasts, with the brigs and schooners raiding inshore and the larger ships lying farther off the coast, out of sight of the shore but within signaling distance. After a final blazing, albeit toothless, salvo at Whydah, the squadron sails southeast to St. Thomas Island (São Tomé), replenishes its supply of Jesuit bark, and then heads back to Freetown. A speedy ten-day passage leaves Aubrey feeling unusually ahead of schedule, until intelligence arrives from Sir Joseph Blaine that the French expedition might also be early.

At last the squadron is in pursuit of French warships, and it cuts a wide swath through the North Atlantic to find them. To the northeast, the *Ringle* finally sights the French invasion force, under Commodore Esprit-Tranquil Maistral, a nonfictional French Naval officer who in 1805 commanded the 84-gun *Neptune* under Villeneuve off Corunna and at Trafalgar. Aubrey's squadron races off in hot pursuit toward the southwest corner of Ireland and Bantry Bay, where the French have made previous unsuccessful attempts to assist Irish insurrections in 1689 and 1796.

HERE AND THERE

Ascension Island

A volcanic island in the South Atlantic Ocean, seven hundred miles northwest of St. Helena. The island was discovered on Ascension Day in 1501 by the Spanish navigator

NEXT PAGE: Aubrey takes his squadron on a much-advertised voyage to the west coast of Africa, where he creates the necessary spectacle. As soon as this is accomplished, he doubles back to intercept a French squadron bound for the southwest coast of Ireland.

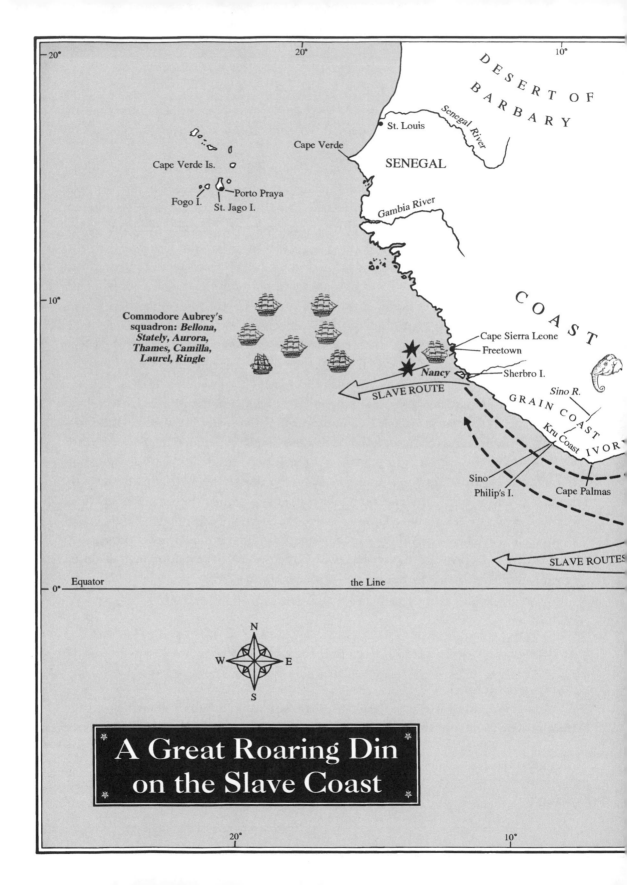

-20°

DESERT OF BARBARY

20°

10°

St. Louis

Senegal River

Cape Verde

SENEGAL

Cape Verde Is.

Porto Praya

Fogo I.   St. Jago I.

Gambia River

-10°

Commodore Aubrey's squadron: *Bellona, Stately, Aurora, Thames, Camilla, Laurel, Ringle*

COAST

Cape Sierra Leone

Freetown

Sino R.

Nancy

Sherbro I.

SLAVE ROUTE

GRAIN COAST

Kru Coast

IVOR

Sino

Philip's I.

Cape Palmas

SLAVE ROUTES

-0°   Equator   the Line

N

W   E

S

A Great Roaring Din on the Slave Coast

20°

10°

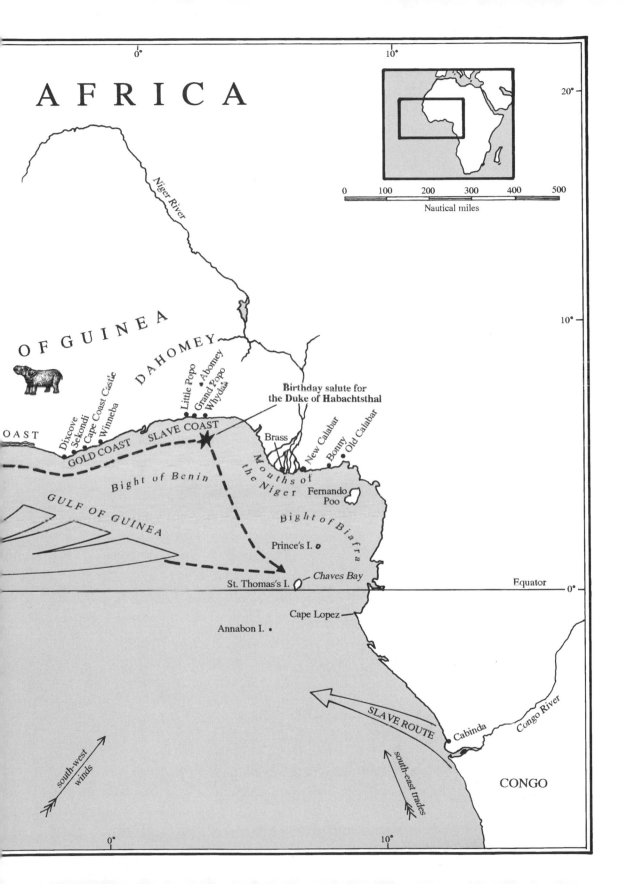

AFRICA

OF GUINEA

Niger River

DAHOMEY

Dixcove
Sekondi
Cape Coast Castle
Winneba
GOLD COAST
COAST
SLAVE COAST

Little Popo
Grand Popo
Abomey
Whydah

**Birthday salute for
the Duke of Habachtsthal**

Brass

New Calabar
Bonny
Old Calabar

Bight of Benin

Mouths of
the Niger

GULF OF GUINEA

Bight of Biafra

Fernando
Poo

Prince's I.

Chaves Bay

St. Thomas's I.

Equator

Cape Lopez

Annabon I.

SLAVE ROUTE

Cabinda

Congo River

south-west
winds

south-east trades

CONGO

0°
10°
20°
10°
0°

0°
10°

100 200 300 400 500
Nautical miles

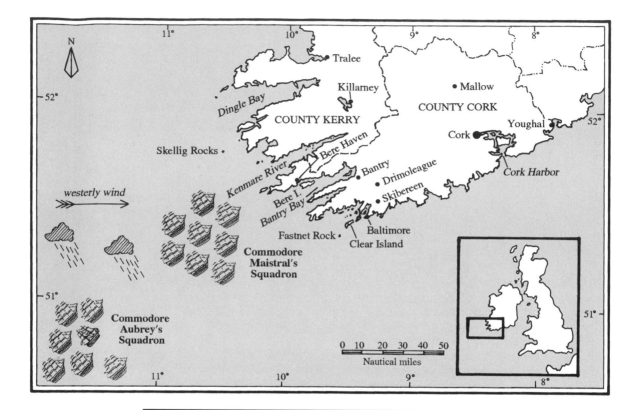

✳ Nabbing the French Near Bantry Bay ✳

Too close to home for comfort, Aubrey and Maturin battle the French at their own doorstep.

Juan de Nova on an expedition for Portugal. Britain established a naval base on the uninhabited island when Napoleon was exiled to St. Helena (1815). The base grew into Georgetown, the main settlement.

Bere Haven
Officially known as Castletown Bearhaven, a small town in County Cork on the north coast of Bantry Bay, with a harbor used as a British Naval base.

Cape Coast Castle
One of more than fifty forts built along the three-hundred-mile Gold Coast (now Ghana) to protect European trade, primarily the slave trade. Cape Coast Castle was

A view of Cape Coast Castle on the Gold Coast of Africa. From Mr. Meredith's "Account of the Gold Coast of Africa": About eight or nine miles east from Elmina, we come to Cape Coast Castle, the headquarters of the British forts and settlements on the Gold Coast and Whidah. It was built by the Portuguese and, with Elmina, ceded to the Dutch, from whom it was taken in 1665. Since then, we have remained in quiet possession of it. . . . The castle is built upon a rock that forms an admirable breastwork towards the south and west and mounts about 90 pieces of cannon, from three- to 36-pounders, with mortars and howitzers. It is not this numerous artillery alone that makes it a place of strength on the seaside; because of shallow water, large ships cannot approach near enough to effect much injury.

Although this Castle presents a formidable appearance towards the sea, it is extremely vulnerable on the land side. It is commanded by high lands, which renders it almost defenseless. . . . The town of Cape Coast is situated immediately in the rear of the castle and extends on each wing to it. Some of the houses overlook the walls, an inconvenience that was not well understood until the year 1803, when the townspeople thought proper to behave ill, which produced a rupture with the castle, the garrison of which was much annoyed with musketry from the tops of those houses. (Spring 1818 edition of *The Naval Chronicle*, p. 221.)

built in 1653 by the Swedes, who called it Cabo Corso. In 1658 it was captured by the Danes, who sold it to the Dutch. The British took control of the fort in 1664 and renamed it Cape Coast Castle. One of the area's primary forts, it could hold up to one thousand slaves at a time.

County Cork

A county in Munster Province in southwest Ireland, on the Atlantic coast. Cork is Ireland's largest county, covering almost three thousand square miles. Its county seat is the city of Cork, which sits at the mouth of the Lee River at the head of Cork Harbour, one of the best natural harbors in Europe. A major seaport is located on Great Island, at the head of the outer harbor. County Cork is home to Blarney Castle, whose famed Blarney Stone is said to endow those who kiss it with the gift of eloquence.

A ship off the southwest coast of Ireland. The annexed plate, engraved by Baily from a drawing by Mr. Pocock, represents HMS *Thunderer* of 74 guns, Captain Bradford, in a storm, off Crookhaven on the night of December 10, 1808. After being nearly wrecked off the Mizen Head, she, by the superior skill and pilotage of the master, Mr. A. Barclay, ran through a narrow pass and anchored safe in Bantry Bay. Crookhaven, on the southwest coast of Ireland, lies in between Cape Clear and Mizen Head. (Spring 1812 edition of *The Naval Chronicle*, p. 318.)

A view of the North Foreland. The isle of Thanet is the northeast promontory of Kent and is separated from the mainland by the river Stour. Ramsgate is a flourishing town of 3,000 inhabitants. Its haven is formed by two piers enclosing a basin of 46 acres with 15-feet depth at high-water neaps, so that it receives vessels of 500 tons. The east coast of England properly commences at the foreland. (Fall 1815 edition of *The Naval Chronicle*, p. 292.)

The Downs

A roadstead and anchorage in the English Channel between the North and South Foreland, about nine miles long and six miles wide, sheltered by the Goodwin Sands, a natural breakwater.

Freetown

An Atlantic seaport and the present-day capital of Sierra Leone. Freetown is located on the shore of a mountainous peninsula that shelters a magnificent natural harbor—the best in western Africa and the third largest in the world. The city was settled in 1787 by liberated slaves under the auspices of British philanthropists.

North Foreland

A one-hundred-foot cliff topped by a distinctive lighthouse on the northeast coast of Kent, England, at the southern end of the Thames estuary. It was off the North Foreland, near the Galloper sandbank, that in 1666, during the Second Dutch War, the Royal Navy fought the Four Days' Battle—one of its most difficult ever—in which it defeated the Dutch but suffered heavy losses.

Sierra Leone

A republic in western Africa, on the Atlantic Ocean. Sierra Leone was inhabited by two native groups—the Temne and the Mende—when it was first visited by Europeans in 1462. The country's name comes from Serra Lyoa ("Lion Mountains"), the name the Portuguese explorer Pedro de Cintra gave to the hills surrounding present-day Freetown.

South Foreland

A three-hundred-foot headland of chalk, three miles northeast of Dover on the coast of southeast Kent, England. The South Foreland's two lighthouses, built about 1620, helped mariners navigate a safe transit south of the treacherous shoals and banks known as the Goodwin Sands, which lay off the coast.

Temple Stairs

Steps leading from the Thames River to the Temple, on its north bank. Because of the sparsity of bridges spanning the Thames before the end of the Napoleonic wars, those Londoners who were not wealthy enough to own their own barges used ferries to cross the river at various landing stages and stairs throughout the city.

Whydah or Ouidah

A seaport on the Gulf of Guinea in Dahomey (present-day Benin). Whydah was founded as a French trading port in the seventeenth century and was a major center of the African slave trade.

Maritime Measures

1 British cable = 608 feet = $\frac{1}{10}$ nautical mile

1 American cable = 720 feet

1 league = 3 statute miles = $\frac{1}{20}$ degree

1 statute mile = 5,280 feet = 320 rods = 1,760 yards = 1.6 kilometers

1 nautical mile = 6,076 feet = 1,852 meters = 1 minute of latitude

1 furlong = $\frac{1}{8}$ statute mile = 40 rods = 220 yards = 201.7 meters

1 degree of latitude = 362,753 feet = 20 leagues = 60 nautical miles

1 fathom = 6 feet = 1.82 meters

1 knot = 1 nautical mile per hour = 1.15 statute miles per hour = 101.27 feet per minute = 1.8 kilometers per hour

Selected Bibliography

In addition to *The Naval Chronicle* and the novels of Patrick O'Brian, the following sources were used in writing this book:

Aldin, Cecil. *The Romance of the Road*. London: Bracken Books, 1986.

Atterby, Paul, ed. *Nicholson's Guide to the Thames: From Source to the Sea*. London: Robert Nicholson Publications, n.d.

Barrow, Sir John. *The Mutiny of the Bounty*. Edited by Gavin Kennedy. Boston: David R. Godine, 1980.

Beaglehole, J. C., ed. *The Journals of Captain Cook*. 4 vols. London: Hakluyt Society, 1955–67.

Bullen, Frank T. *The Cruise of the Cachalot: Round the World after Sperm Whales*. New York: D. Appleton and Company, 1899.

Callow, Edward. *Old London Taverns: Historical, Descriptive and Reminiscent*. New York: Brentano's, 1901.

Clout, Hugh, ed. *The Times London History Atlas*. New York: HarperCollins, 1991.

Cotter, C. H. *A History of Nautical Astronomy*. London: Hollis and Carter, 1968.

Cruising Association. *The Cruising Association Handbook*. 3d ed. London: Cruising Association, 1971.

Cunningham, A. E., ed. *Patrick O'Brian: Critical Essays and a Bibliography*. New York: Norton, 1994.

Dann, John C., ed. *The Nagle Journal: A Diary of the Life of Jacob Nagle, Sailor, from the Year 1775 to 1841*. New York: Weidenfeld and Nicolson, 1988.

Darby, H. C., and Harold Fullard. *The New Cambridge Modern History.* Vol. 14, *Atlas.* Cambridge: Cambridge University Press, 1970.

David, Andrew, ed. *The Charts and Coastal Views of Captain Cook's Voyages.* 2 vols. London: Hakluyt Society, 1988, 1992.

Duncan, T. Bentley. *Atlantic Islands: Madeira, the Azores and the Cape Verdes in Seventeenth-Century Commerce and Navigation.* Chicago: University of Chicago Press, 1972.

Edwards, Ruth Dudley. *An Atlas of Irish History.* 2d ed. New York: Methuen, 1981.

Fayle, C. Ernest, et al. *The Trade Winds: A Study of British Overseas Trade During the French Wars 1793–1815.* Edited by C. Northcote Parkinson. London: George Allen and Unwin Ltd., 1948.

Findlay, Alexander George. *A Directory for the North Atlantic Ocean.* London: Richard Holmes Laurie, 1894.

Gilbert, Martin. *British History Atlas.* London: Weidenfeld and Nicolson, 1968.

Hattendorf, John B., ed. *Maritime History.* 2 vols. Melbourne, Fla.: Kreiger Publishing, 1996.

Hattendorf, John B., et al., eds. *British Naval Documents, 1204–1960.* London: Navy Records Society, 1993.

Hewson, J. B. *A History of the Practice of Navigation.* Glasgow: Brown, Son and Ferguson, 1951.

Hill, Richard. *The Oxford Illustrated History of the Royal Navy.* Oxford and New York: Oxford University Press, 1995.

Howse, Derek. *Greenwich Time and the Discovery of Longitude.* Oxford: Oxford University Press, 1980.

Hydrographer of the Navy. *The English Channel Handbook.* London: Hydrographic Office, 1943.

———. *Mediterranean Pilot.* London: Hydrographic Department, 1965.

———. *Ocean Passages for the World.* Taunton, England: Hydrographic Department, 1973.

Kemp, Peter, ed. *The Oxford Companion to Ships and the Sea.* Oxford: Oxford University Press, 1993.

Kerhallet, Ch. Philippe, Imperial French Navy. *General Examination of the Atlantic Ocean.* Translated by R. H. Wyman, U.S. Navy. Washington, D.C.: Government Printing Office, 1870.

———. *General Examination of the Indian Ocean.* Translated by R. H. Wyman, U.S. Navy. Washington, D.C.: Government Printing Office, 1870.

Le Gras, A. *General Examination of the Mediterranean Sea: A Summary of Its Winds, Currents, and Navigation.* Translated by R. H. Wyman, U.S. Navy. Washington, D.C.: Government Printing Office, 1870.

Mackesy, Piers. *The War in the Mediterranean: 1803–1810.* Cambridge, Mass.: Harvard University Press, 1957.

Marryat, Frederick. *Peter Simple.* New York: Dutton, 1974.

Nordhoff, Charles, and James Norman Hall. *Mutiny on the Bounty.* New York: Pocket Books, 1970.

———. *Botany Bay.* Boston: Little, Brown and Company, 1941.

Parkinson, C. Northcote. *War in the Eastern Seas: 1793–1815.* London: George Allen and Unwin Ltd., 1954.

Porter, A. N., ed. *Atlas of British Overseas Expansion.* New York: Simon and Schuster, 1991.

Pryor, John H. *Geography, Technology, and War: Studies in the Maritime History of the Mediterranean, 649–1571.* Cambridge: Cambridge University Press, 1988.

Rienits, Rex and Thea. *The Voyages of Captain Cook.* London: Paul Hamlyn, 1968.

Ritchie, G. S. *The Admiralty Chart: British Naval Hydrography in the Nineteenth Century.* Rev. ed. Edinburgh: The Pentland Press, 1995.

Sawyer, F. E. *Sailing Directions of the Indian Ocean.* Washington, D.C.: Government Printing Office, 1887.

Spruner, K. von, and Th. Menke, eds. *Spruner-Menke Hand-Atlas für die Geschichte des Mittelalters und der Neuern Zeit*, 3rd ed. Gotha: Justus Perthes, 1880.

Taylor, E. G. R. *The Haven Finding Art.* New York: Abelard-Schuman, 1957.

Taylor, E. G. R., and M. W. Richey. *The Geometrical Seaman: A Book of Early Nautical Instruments.* London: Hollis and Carter for the Institute of Navigation, 1962.

Uden, Grant, and Richard Cooper. *A Dictionary of British Ships and Seamen.* New York: St. Martin's Press, 1980.

Villiers, Alan. *Voyaging with the Wind.* London: Her Majesty's Stationery Office, 1975.

Waters, D. W. "The English Pilot: English Sailing Directions and Charts and the Rise of English Shipping." *Journal of Navigation* 42 (1989): 317–54.

Watson, J. Steven. *The Reign of George III: 1760–1815.* Oxford: Clarendon Press, 1960.

Wyman, R. H. *Winds, Currents, and Navigation of the Gulf of Cadiz, the Western Coast of the Spanish Peninsula, and the Strait of Gibraltar.* Washington, D.C.: Government Printing Office, 1870.

Index

If you would like to discuss issues concerning *Harbors and High Seas* or the geography of the Aubrey-Maturin novels, please write to:

Editor, *Harbors and High Seas*
Henry Holt and Co., Inc.
115 West 18th St.
New York, NY 10011

Or you can contact the author directly by e-mail at:

DeanHKing@aol.com